Rockie

The Discovery, Excavation and Preservation of a Prehistoric Bison, Burnet County, Texas

Edited by Thomas R. Hester

Publication No. 1
The Falls on the Colorado Museum
Marble Falls, TX

2023

Copyright © 2023
By The Falls of the Colorado Museum
Published By NorTex Press
An Imprint of Wild Horse Media Group
P.O. Box 331779
Fort Worth, Texas 76163
1-817-344-7036
www.WildHorseMedia.com
ALL RIGHTS RESERVED
Paperback ISBN-13: 978-1-68179-356-6
Hardback ISBN-13: 978-1-68179-357-3
Ebook ISBN-13: 978-1-68179-358-0

ALL RIGHTS RESERVED. No part of this book may be reproduced in any form without written permission from the publisher, except for brief passages included in a review appearing in a newspaper or magazine.

Printed in the United States of America.

The FALLS on the COLORADO museum

Mission Statement

To preserve our history,
To further our heritage,
To protect artifacts, and
To provide an ongoing history of Marble Falls and the surrounding communities.

Board Members 2023

Amanda Seim
Darlene Oostermeyer
Marianne Holland McEwin
Nancy Ebeling
Danielle Meredith
Dr. Jane Knapik
Rev. George Perry
Sharon Spencer
Marley Porter
Vashti Tucker
Dr. Thomas Hester
Ron Nicholas
George Russell
Robyn Richter

PO BOX 1333 MARBLE FALLS, TX 78654 | 830.798.2157 |
FOCMUSEUMCHAIR@GMAIL.COM
2001 BROADWAY MARBLE FALLS, TX (PHYSICAL) | FALLSMUSEUM.ORG

TABLE OF CONTENTS

Foreword: A Simple Email and 13 Boxes of Bones
   Darlene Oostermeyer 7

Studying Rockie: An Introduction
   Thomas R. Hester 11

Bison Archaeology in Texas
   Harry J. Shafer 13

Rockie, the Briggs Bison: Notes from the Finder's Journal
   Ryan Murray 21

Rockie: A Late Prehistoric Bison Kill in Burnet County, Texas
   David L. Calame, Sr., Ryan Murray and Raymond Mauldin 37

Body Size of the Rocky Creek Site Bison, Burnet County, Texas, USA: Context and Explanations
   Jeff M. Martin 43

Rockie's Preparation
   Kenneth Bader 51

List of Authors 57

Foreword

A Simple Email and 13 Boxes of Bones

Darlene Oostermeyer

It is amazing how one simple email and one conversation can change a museum! This email brought an instant breath of fresh air that lifted our spirit and helped lead a group in a wonderful direction.

That simple email from Ryan Murray to Board of Directors member Dr. Tom Hester, dated October 26, 2016, was a catalyst for The Falls on the Colorado Museum to develop its natural history room. Dr. Tom cornered me in front of our display cases containing marvelous Native American artifacts from the Central Texas area. When he mentioned acquiring the bones of a 700-year-old bison from Ryan, we immediately knew we needed to say "Yes!" I knew that there would be immediate support from the Board and the community, and there was.

Soon after this conversation, 13 large boxes of bison bones were delivered by Ryan. The skull was in great shape, and we knew it needed to be displayed immediately. Ryan's family had christened the bison

as "Rockie" as a tribute to the Burnet County stream on which she was found: Rocky Creek.

A local artisan, the "wood whisperer" Ken McBride had just completed the amazing Mormon Mill exhibit for the Museum. It was a work of art that was both an incredible display and an unbelievable educational tool. We immediately contacted Ken to scope out the skull and how best it could be displayed fairly quickly. Ken rose to the task and replied "Yes" as soon as he saw Rockie's skull.

A month later, Ken delivered a magnificent display case that became the resting place for her skull. This case had been made of 250 year-old cypress wood to which I donated 100 year-old longleafed pine and pecan wood from my grandparents' home nearby. Ken took the additional wood to his home workshop, returning weeks later with another masterpiece display cabinet.

During the time Ken worked on the skull display, Dr. Tom had secured the services of Kenny Bader who was a fossil preparator at the Vertebrate Paleontology Laboratory (VPL), a part of the Jackson School of Geosciences at UT-Austin. Kenny agreed take on the task of repairing the bison bones in his spare time.

Dr. Tom and I had discussed how best to display Rockie, and I had my heart set on posing her vertically, as if she was standing on the grassy Llano Estacado. Both Dr. Tom and Kenny felt her bones were too fragile for that orientation. Another basic reason my pipedream was shattered was that almost all of Rockie's lower bones were missing as a result of erosion in the creek, flooding over time and erosion when exposed to the elements. (Another statement will be made on this dilemma later.)

Concurrent with displaying Rockie's skull, we began fundraising. First, we designed a "Rockie gauge" to show our progress in money raised to-date. Visitors, both local and out-of-towners, were quite generous. It was so much fun to watch kids come in to see Rockie's skull and put change from their piggy banks in the donation jar!

The museum worked extremely hard obtaining grants that would help defray the costs associated with reconstruction of Rockie and the larger display case that would eventually be needed when those 13 boxes of bones became almost an entire skeleton.

I discovered from Dr. Dan McBride, a beloved veterinarian in Burnet that a local taxidermist Robert Griffith would be butchering a three year-old bull from his bison herd. I asked Robert if the museum could have the carcass so that we could use the lower extremities to complete Rockie's missing leg bones. Robert agreed to give us the carcass, minus the head which he planned to mount.

Kenny Bader had agreed to put the bulls' legs in the "bug room" at the VPL. This allowed the dermestid beetle colony there to scour the bones removing the soft tissue. On a hot Fall day, Robert called saying he had culled the bull and that the carcass was available. He also mentioned that we should bring several large construction trash bags to transport the remains. My husband Tom and I headed north to Burnet. Nothing could have prepared me for what I saw on the taxidermist's floor! The bloody carcass filled four, maybe five, 42-gallon trash bags! I swear on the way back to Marble Falls we had a cloud of flies following our pickup. We met Kenny at the museum and transferred the bags to the back of his Jeep Cherokee. At that time, Kenny's AC was out in his Jeep, but he contended if he drove fast enough back to Austin, he could outrun the fly swarm!

After Kenny saw the size of the bull's lower leg bones, he confirmed that using those bones in the Rockie exhibit would make Rockie look as if she had "training wheels" for legs. The bull's bones were unbelievably smaller than Rockie's leg bones would have been! Now I understood why Rockie would need to be displayed horizontally as she had been uncovered on the banks of Rocky Creek.

Throughout all this time, the museum continued to fundraise until completion in June

2017. The City of Marble Falls and Burnet County were very supportive and generous. Our efforts to raise money did have some wonderful highs and some disappointing lows. At one time, I prepared 17 personal letters to companies and individuals located in the area. I hand-carried these letters to the appropriate people and even chatted with them about our efforts. Of the 17 requests for contributions, we received only two responses. Fortunately, several grants were awarded for Rockie's reconstruction and display case and we thus obtained adequate funding to meet all our obligations. All of our professional help and master carpentry work was done at a steep discount so that we would be successful.

Meanwhile, Rockie's skull was tantalizing folks! "It's so big" we kept hearing. I had recently seen a modern bison bull "nibble" on my pickup truck's side mirror while I was at our family cemetery. I had my windows open and realized his head would not fit in the open window. Luckily, he sauntered off since I didn't disturb the nearby cow and calf, but I realized how huge he really was. This too close and personal observation made me begin to wonder just how large Rockie's skeleton was going to be.

About this same time, wood whisperer Ken wondered if we had final dimensions for the big display case. I called Kenny who suggested Dr. Tom, Ken and I meet him at the museum to lay out some bones to gauge the final dimensions. We put down an old quilt on the floor, and Kenny started arranging bones. All of us were shocked; Rockie was almost eight feet long!

We decided as a team that a structure at least 10 feet long would be needed and the display level would need to be about three feet off the floor. We also knew the case would need glass all around so that Rockie could be viewed from any place in the room. Ken went back to his workshop and assembled a 10'6" long x 5'6" high x 5'6" deep modular display, one so beautiful that it alone is a work of art. It took Ken and 3 helpers several days to assemble the showcase in one of our old school rooms. The case had to be turned on the diagonal so that the weight of the case and Rockie would be distributed across the old floor which has no subfloor. Additionally, we had to provide for sufficient space for wheelchairs to move around the case.

Then came the day of reckoning: assembling all the bones. Kenny and I had spent hours loading playground sand in the case, almost 50 bags, to raise the sand up to the glass level so sightlines were not diminished. Our hours were extended when I had to make two extra trips to the local big box store for more sand.

When Kenny moved the skull from the smaller display case and positioned it in the big case, Rockie's skull disappeared in the sand. Her bones were almost the same color as the play sand, which was a showstopper. Kenny called on his vast experiences with other displays and suggested we top the play sand with garnet sand. I just stared at him wondering where in the world we would find garnet sand in Marble Falls, Texas. Quite a few phone calls later, we located a man who lives at the north end of Lake Buchanan and uses garnet sand for sand blasting. He sold us 10 bags on the spot and at a discounted price. We rushed back to the museum where Kenny topped off the play sand with nine bags of the garnet sand. When Kenny reset Rockie's skull, it was a perfect contrast color to make her skeleton stand out. Many hours later, nearing midnight, the last of the bones were in place, and Rockie came to life for us.

Another Board member Krissy Sralla and I wrote a script to accompany a video put together by Ben Friberg and Ricardo Ruano depicting how Rockie was stumbled upon by Ryan and dug up with friends, reconstructed by Kenny, and housed in Ken's beautiful showcase. Once the video was completed, my neighbor Ray Murphy who is a radio announcer, volunteered to voice over our script. Voila, and the video was done. Once again, Ken built another stellar case for the TV and CD drive using the very last of the wood scraps. We were ready to show Rockie to the town!

Another major display we had made in the original case that housed the skull is an exhibit that compares the massive bones of Rockie to a less than massive modern bull bison.

We chose to display Rockie in the position she was discovered on the bank of Rocky Creek, buried by 6-8 feet of overburden and 6-8 feet above the water line when found. The overburden had to be carefully removed so that the team could work from makeshift scaffolding suspended above the creek. Her left side bones are laid out in the underneath compartment of the display case.

Unveiling Rockie occurred on October 13, 2018. Ryan, his family, his helpers, and as many of the other folks we could get, were guests of honor. Ryan was the first person allowed in the room to view Miss Rockie in all her glory.

Since that unveiling, Rockie's display continues to amaze folks about how far south the North American bison once roamed. We also educate visitors to the difference between North American bison and Asian Water Buffalo and Cape Buffalo.

What a treasure those 13 boxes of bones were to The Falls on the Colorado Museum!

STUDYING ROCKIE: AN INTRODUCTION

Thomas R. Hester

This publication, the first from The Falls on the Colorado Museum, appears on the 10th anniversary of the discovery of "Rockie." Rockie is the name given to a female bison skeleton found by Ryan Murray in 2013, eroding from a creek bank near Briggs, in northeastern Burnet County. The all-volunteer excavation that followed has led to the involvement of the museum in the preservation and exhibition of this archaeological find.

The contributions to this volume include a Foreword by Darlene Oostermeyer who served as chair of the Board of Directors at the time this work was carried out, and with great enthusiasm she took on the task of raising the funds for the preservation and exhibit. Dr. Harry J. Shafer has generously provided an overview of the role of bison in the prehistory of the indigenous Native American peoples in Texas. He provides his observations on the role of climate in the spread of bison herds at different periods of time during prehistory. He examines the hunting technology, the chipped stone artifacts linked to hunting and butchering and the overall importance of the bison to the ancient peoples of the region. In Ryan Murray's "Journal", he provides his personal views of finding and excavating Rockie. He describes the problems and difficulties involved, the role of his family and the work of the volunteer crew. His article reflects the dedication and the excitement of the excavation. The donation of Rockie's skeleton to the museum, the preservation of the bones and the construction and installation of the exhibit were all part of Ryan's experience.

The following article by David Calame, Ryan Murray, and Raymond Mauldin reviews the logistics of the excavations and the careful study of a Perdiz arrow point found in the chest cavity of the bison. This served to show that hunting caused the death of the animal. Raymond Mauldin presents a convincing case, with the necessary technical language, of the time of Rockie's demise around A.D. 1347.

The intense and technically detailed study of a calcaneum (the heel bone) was done by Dr. Jeff M. Martin, a specialist in bison research at South Dakota State University. He describes what the data reveal about the climate, the size and weight of this bison, along with other details. His work integrates his finding about Rockie into a set of skeletal remains that illuminate our knowledge of North American bison in the 14th century

Paleontologist Ken Bader carried out the long hours of cleaning, conserving and restoring Rockie's skeleton. He then prepared and systematicaly arranged the bones for installation in what is a major permanent exhibit of the museum. His article details the painstaking work done by a skilled preparator on a step by step basis.

The many aspects of finding a well preserved bison whose death, around A.D. 1347, resulted from Native American hunting episode, gives us a rare glimpse of a specific event in prehistory. However, as the authors note, there remains a question as to whether marks found on some of the bones are indicative of butchering marks—cuts made by stone knives. Rockie's skeleton was certainly not disarticulated as is often seen in the typical butchering patterns of bison.

In the future, as new techniques of study continue to develop, more questions can be asked of the bones, revealing new information and indeed new perspectives we have not thought of today. With the curation provided by the museum, these bones will long be available for study. The events of ancient human lifeways are not wholly revealed at one site, or one excavation, or in one series of technical analyses. Archaeology requires scientific documentation of the past, but its overarching role is to explain the patterns of prehistory in a broad and meaningful manner.

ACKNOWLEDGMENTS

I want to thank all of the authors for their contributions to this publication. Amanda Seim and Darlene Oostermeyer provided much needed review of the final drafts of the submitted manuscripts. Darlene Oostermeyer is greatly thanked for her tremendous work in securing the donation of Rockie, raising the needed funds for conservation of the bones and the exhibit of the restored remains. She further encouraged the completion and publication of these studies. Indeed, the cover is her concept, designed by Eric Teague (Signs2Go). Terry Sherrel, graphic designer, formatted the text and designed the publication. I think Rockie is pleased!

BISON ARCHAEOLOGY IN TEXAS

Harry J. Shafer

INTRODUCTION

American Indians hunting bison on a horse is an iconic image in the minds of many people when they think of Indians or bison. Truthfully, this is only a fleeting image in time and geography; the horse was not adopted by the Indians of the Plains until about 1650 AD at a time when bison were ranging from Texas to the Great Plains.

Moving back in time in central Texas, bison were only present at certain times in prehistory, but when they were, they provided an economic boom to the Indians. I use the phrase, walking WalMarts, to describe the importance of bison to the Indians of Texas; not one scrap of the bison went to waste. Bison were not indigenous to central Texas like whitetail deer; they did range into central Texas and were present from time to time, they just did not stay. To understand why, a look at several factors that occurred since the last Ice Age provides an interesting correlation on the coming and going of these hefty creatures.

CLIMATE, PRAIRIE EVOLUTION, BISON EVOLUTION

There were three factors that came together that were responsible for the appearance of bison in central Texas, and for their absence: climate, evolution of the prairie, and bison evolution. First was climate. Following the last ice age around 11,500 B.P, the climate became gradually warmer and dryer in central Texas. Bison were absent and the main large animal hunted was the whitetail deer. But given the absence of such food stocks as the bison, the Archaic people turned to exploiting

Figure 1. Stereotypical image of an Indian hunting bison (Amon Carter Museum: Charlie Russell, The Bison Hunt #39)

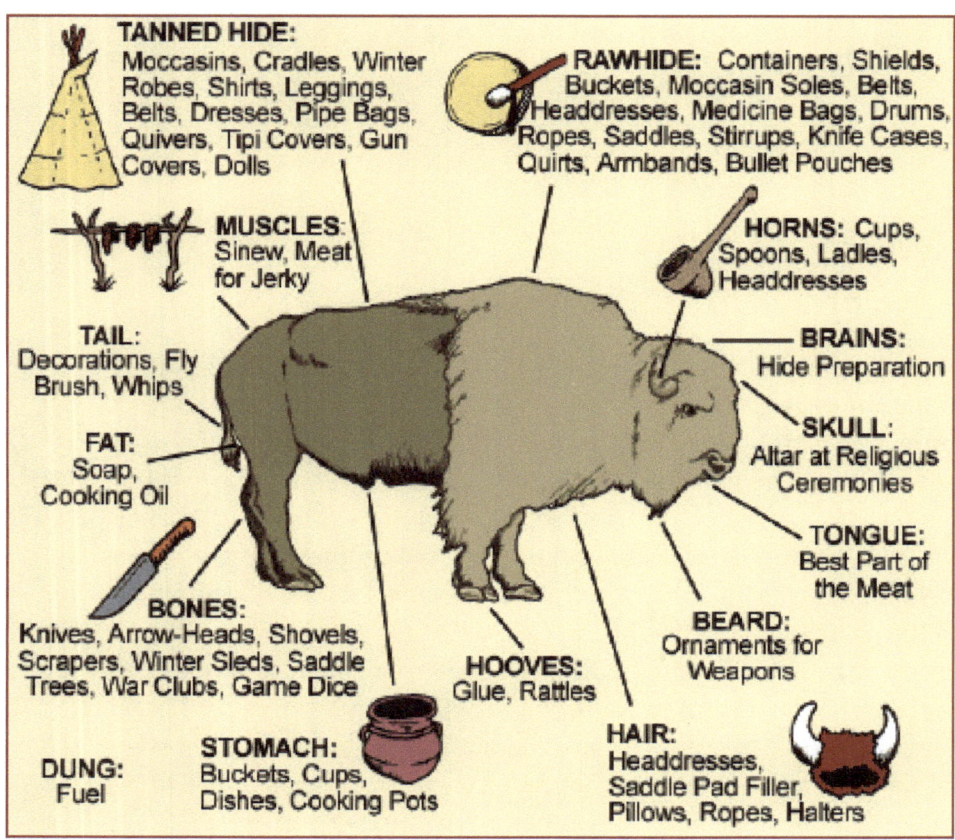

Figure 2. Use was made of every part of the bison, to the Indians of Texas, they were like a walking Walmart® (Graphic image from South Dakota State Historical Society).

smaller game and the local plant communities. Archaeologists begin finding the evidence of hot rock cooking and earth ovens after about 10,000 B.P. Deer, small game such as rabbits, and the slowest creature on the landscape, *Rabdotus* land snails, were some of the protein sources.

About 6,000-5,000 BP, however, the climate became a bit cooler and wetter, and since it was probably much colder in the High Plains, bison moved southward into Texas. Or, perhaps the grazing was better. This is the Calf Creek archaeological horizon identified by the heavily-barbed Calf Creek (Andice) and Bell spear points. These animals were B*ison antiquus* and *B. occidentalis* that had survived from the end of the Pleistocene.

Over time stress on the bison during the Holocene and the evolution of the Great Plains environment led to smaller body size and smaller horns. The climate became dry again for nearly 3,000 years before another cold wet cycle occurred about 3,500 BP. And again, bison returned. The evolution of the Great Plains now was covered with drought resistant short grasses. Some relate this grassland evolution to bison evolution. During this time *Bison bison*, modern bison, migrated to Texas and became heavily exploited to the extent that the regional economies of the natives changed significantly. As bison became more common and heavily hunted, a technology was created to adjust to this new resource.

Bison once again moved out of Texas about 2,000 years ago or slightly later, leaving whitetail deer as the animal of choice. Evidence from the Balcones edge shows deer to have been exploited particularly for hides, and hunted with the corner notched Marcos and Ensor spear points. Small corner-tang knives continued to be used and traded to people along the coastal plain.

Bison exited central Texas at the onset of the Medieval Warm Period during the Austin phase that lasted from about A. D. 700-1200. Interestingly, this also was about the time that the bow and arrow became the weapon of choice. Corner-notched Scallorn and Sabinal replaced the thicker Darl spear points. In the northern part of central Texas Bonham arrow points and Gahagan knives were the major diagnostics. Scallorn was the earlier of the two arrow points styles with Bonham appearing around A. D. 1100, possibly co-occurring with Scallorn. Interaction with the Caddo to the east also resulted in the first appearance of trade pottery in central Texas.

The onset of the Little Ice Age just prior to A. D. 1300 saw bison once again appearing in central Texas, this time apparently in great numbers. The common tool kit was the heavily-barbed Perdiz arrow points, end scrapers, beveled knives, small delicate drills, and bone tempered pottery. Bison were present well into the Historic period based on multiple accounts by Spanish explorers and missionaries.

TECHNOLOGY

When bison were present in the region so were artifacts indicative of their exploitation. The interesting fact about prehistoric technology and bison hunting was the need for heavily barbed spear, and later arrow points. When bison were present from ca. 6,000 to 5,000 BP, the heavily barbed Calf Creek (Andice) and Bell points were preferred. When bison were absent, the lanceolate or lightly shouldered Nolan points seemed to be the preference. At the time of their arrival Pedernales spear points were the regional norm, but the slender forms may have become restyled to barbed examples as barbed spear points are generally associated with bison exploitation. During the Late Archaic, 3,000-2,000 B.P., diagnostics included barbed Marshall, Castroville, and Montell. The Toyah Interval is identified by heavily-barbed Perdiz arrow points. Why the need for barbs? Perhaps they were considered more lethal, or possibly by staying in the animal the ownership of the carcass or part of it could be claimed based on personal identity marked on the shafts. Arrows, and probably spears had personal markings, either painting or incising.

Figure 3. Right, Calf Creek (Andice) left, and Bell spear points.

Other artifacts that were part of the bison hunting tool kit included end scrapers for hide processing and expedient and curated knives for butchering. Expedient knives were generally flakes with extremely sharp feather terminations that were simply handheld for fine cutting. Once the task was done, they were discarded. Archaeologists often overlook these artifacts entirely or relegate them to "utilized flakes." Microscopic use wear could relate the wear to butchering. Curated knives included corner tangs, base tangs, and oval or subtriangular forms in the Archaic. The four-edge and two-edge beveled knives of the Toyah Interval were highly curated, that is hafted and carried from place to place; they were resharpened by unifacial retouch until beveled edges ceased to be functional and the knives were discarded. Another interesting knife that co-occurs with Castroville and Montell in some parts of the Hill Country are butted knives (Kerrville bifaces, Turner et al. 2011:235). These interesting tools were handheld and had fine cutting blades and rounded tips.

Hunting strategies are largely unknown in central Texas, but this might be due to archaeologists looking in the wrong places. Well known bison drive sites such as Bonfire Shelter in the lower Pecos clearly reveal that strategy, but how open land hunting was done is unknown. My personal view is that bison drives were far more common than our current evidence shows. This view is based on the location of sites such as Eagle Bluff in Medina County that has a bison hide processing area very near the steep bluff that overlooks Hondo Creek. Kill site evidence would have been washed away by the creek, during periods of high velocity flooding. Similar situations occur in Bell County. One such site is where a bluff overlooks Nolan Creek. A large Late Archaic site with Castroville, Montell, bison bone (teeth), and corner tang knives is on a creek terrace near the bluff. Another Toyah Interval site, notable for bison bone, Leon Plain and Caddo pottery, is adjacent to a prominent bluff overlooking the creek. Archaeologists could well consider such advantageous localities at or near sites where bison era components occur.

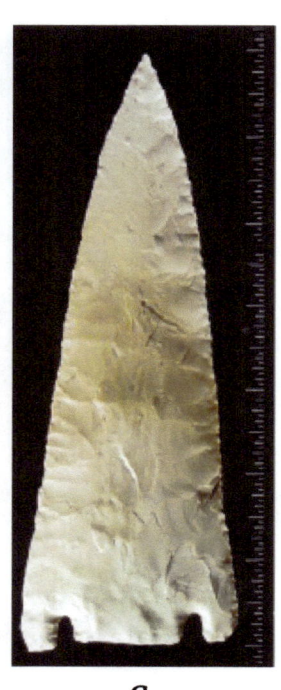

Figure 4. Castroville and Montell spear points, base tang, and corner tang knives. A, Castroville; B, Montell; C, base-tang (San Saba) knife; D, corner-tang knife.

ECONOMY

The idea that bison would be preferred over deer is understandable. This change would probably necessitate a shift in settlement pattern for more mobility in order to pursue the animals. Deer and pronghorn were not forgotten but were no longer the focus. Bison hides and jerked meat carried considerable weight economically and would have given any group who had such resources great bargaining opportunities. Other major economic resources were red and yellow ochre and artifacts of Edwards chert (particularly large knives and spear points.) In return, seashells, especially conch shell beads, pendants, and gorgets, were highly sought after items along with feathers from large migratory birds. Caddo pottery was one of the items coming from east Texas, evidence of Caddo interaction, either carried by Caddo joining local groups on the hunt, as trade items, or as Caddo women joining central Texas groups. Evidence of these durable artifacts going their respective ways is confirmed archaeologically. Undoubtedly, other items were exchanged that do not appear or are not identified in the archaeological record.

The exchange of bison goods was facilitated by trading fairs organized at major gathering places and attended by tribal groups from near and far. These events were as much social as economic and provided the opportunities for not only material exchange but also marriages and other forms of group mixing and alliance building.

SUMMARY

In conclusion, one can imagine the surprise and importance of bison showing up one morning to a hunter-gatherer group. Having subsisted on rabbits, snails, and river mussels with an occasional deer kill for most of one's life, barely keeping warm in the cold winter nights, and then seeing a source for most of your needs walking by must have been quite a pleasant shock!

Suddenly their life and economy changed. As the cold intervals began to occur, there was a source for warm hides and plenty of food. The presence of bison may have lasted several generations, enough to gain the attention of friends and enemies alike. Material wealth was now possible. Surplus bison products became an important source of barter with poorer have-not groups; also, territorial encroachment from uninvited neighbors seeking opportunities for themselves expectedly led to violent encounters, a consequence of having bison in one's midst.

Figure 5. A, Perdiz arrow points; B, four-edge beveled knife.

Figure 6. Bonfire Mural by Nola Montgomery, Texas Parks and Wildlife Department, original on display at Seminole Canyon State Park. Bonfire is a Paleoinion bision drive site near Langtry.

Hunters and gatherers, by definition, lived off the land but the lands were not equal, nor were they unchanging. People adapted and adjusted their cultures accordingly. Certainly, archaeology has recorded evidence of adaptation and adjustments when bison were present, only to adjust their culture accordingly when there were no bison.

REFERENCE CITED

Turner, E. S., T. R. Hester and R. L. McReynolds
2011 *Stone Artifacts of Texas Indians*. 3rd edition. Taylor Trade Publishing, Rowman and Littlefield, Lanham, Maryland.

Figure 1. Aerial view of the excavations. Note the parked cars of the volunteers.

ROCKIE, THE BRIGGS BISON: NOTES FROM THE FINDER'S JOURNAL

Ryan Murray

INTRODUCTION

Documentation of an almost complete bison ("buffalo") skeleton excavation was done in the spring of 2014 at a locale on South Rocky Creek in northeast Burnet County, Texas. This location is between Briggs and the unincorporated town of Watson. Radiocarbon dating revealed the adult animal lived in prehistoric times around 700 years ago (1301-1406 A.D.). The area is part of a large migration corridor that stretched down the continent, through the Great Plains and into the Edwards Plateau. This bison was a 1300-1800 pound, seven-year old female at time of death in the Lampasas River drainage basin. The time period is about 300 years before European contact, a time when interbreeding occurred between cattle and the American bison. Small broken pieces of flint were found in the soil excavated within the skeleton's torso, along with a shattered arrow point. There are some indications that the bones have cut marks suggesting that there may have been butchering by prehistoric hunters.

The following passages from my journal will give some measure of the excitement and anticipation of the bison excavation. The bison was named "Rockie" by my family during the excavations. Later, I donated the skeleton to The Falls of the Colorado Museum in Marble Falls, where it was restored and is now exhibited.

THE JOURNAL

1/15/14

In late summer of 2013 while visiting my favorite fishing hole on the family ranch, I was walking north downstream on the east bank of South Rocky Creek and spotted a small white protrusion in the creek bank about the size and shape of a piece of chalk, lying flush with the cutbank. After a little digging, I realized it was a large bone and it appeared to be very old. It was buried deep and I was not able to remove it! I returned to the site the following week to try to exhume the rest of it and realized that it was a large ulna and that there were more bones present. I came back several times over the following weeks and collected some of the ribs and leg bones, although at the time I was unsure what type of animal it was.

Early on, I took some of the bones to Morris Bussey, the "Fossil Guy" who owns an eccentric and sublime rock shop in Glen Rose and he thought they were prehistoric whalebones. Later I brought an ulna to the Vertebrate Paleontology Laboratory (VPL) at The University of Texas at Austin. The staff there told me I had bison bones, and after examining the condition and hearing my description of the

> "I realized it was a large bone and it appeared to be very old."

A

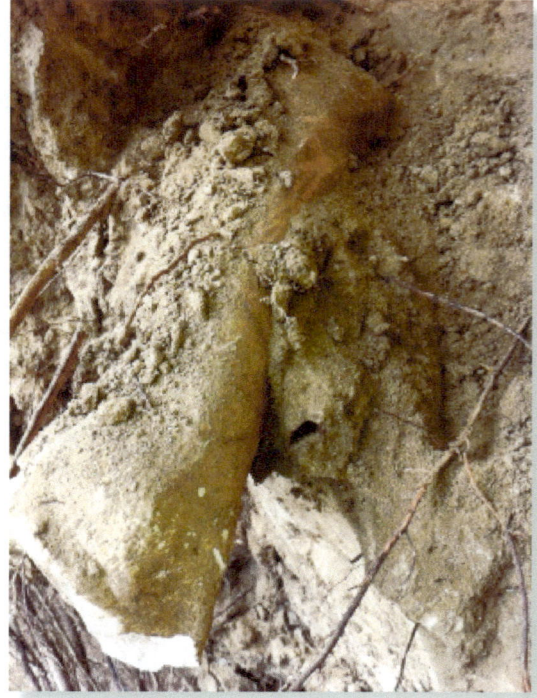

B

Figure 2. A, The creek bank, and B, after brushing away some soil matrix and recognizing the large bone.

Figure 3. the initial appearance of the area in which Rockie was excavated.

context, their estimate on possible age range was between 2,000 and 10,000 years. That was in October 2013 and at the time I had exhumed two radius bones, two ulnae, and some rib fragments. The ribs were extremely fragile and broke easily, so I decided not to dig further. Around this time, my family decided to name the animal "Rockie" after Rocky Creek.

In November 2013, the site was extremely difficult to access. I spent several days cutting brush with loppers and chainsaws to remove the shrubbery and juniper trees above the site. I removed large amounts of thorned ivy and tree roots, as well as a foot of topsoil humus. There was a barbed wire fence that was right on top of the site that had to be removed. The neighbors have told us the fence has been there for 75-100 years and the wires went directly through the trunk of a large tree that had grown around it. My friends Todd and Geoff Johnson helped in this initial site preparation, along with my father Duane and wife Jessica. Here is a drawing I made around that time:

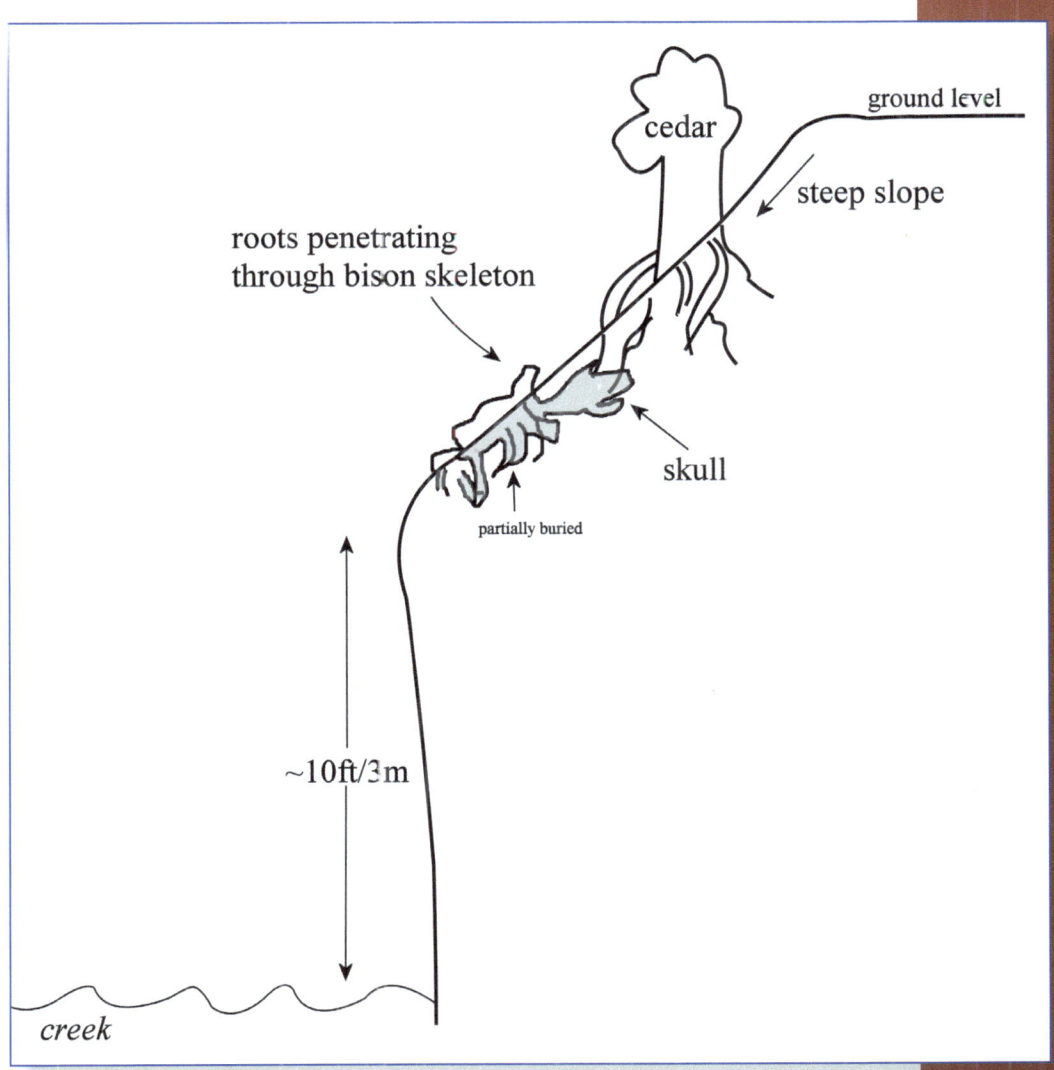

Figure 4. Profile sketch of the Rockie locality. Redrawn by Lance K. Trask.

> *The bones were wet and brittle.*

1/7/14

My cousin Seth Baldwin joined me on November 9-10, 2013 to dig. We exhumed more of the ribs and the coxae (bones of the pelvic girdle), and bagged and labeled everything.

The bones were wet and brittle. Our layman's inexperience would probably make a professional archaeologist or paleontologist cringe, as our clumsiness and naïveté caused minor superficial damage to the specimen. The precarious position and the skeleton's orientation were also difficult to overcome. At one point during this weekend, Seth was standing on the scaffold, suspended over the creek with ropes tied to trees. I was on the northeastern upstream end of the skeleton and Dad was up the hill above me by four or five feet. Dad leaned on a dead branch of a cedar tree above us, and Seth and I were standing on the sloped ledge when the branch gave out and sent Dad tumbling face-first down the hill to the creek's vertical shear wall. The branch, about six inches thick, swung around like a baseball bat, hit me in the back and knocked the wind out of me. His fall was broken by another cedar post—this one having been part of the barbed wire fence that some unsuspecting mender had driven into the ground some 100 or so years prior. The posthole was bored to within a few inches shy of drilling right into the coxae of the skeleton. The post caught Dad (rather than the other way around) and saved the three of us from avalanching into the stony creek bed 12 feet below! In the end, we were breathing a sigh of relief and were able to laugh at the bumbling clumsiness of what could have potentially caused substantial injury to any one of us.

Figure 5. Initial exposure of the bison rib cage.

At another point in the site preparation, I was chain sawing a tree trunk and as it fell, the branches hit the ground awkwardly and it recoiled back at me. It ripped my shirt wide open and punched my abdomen hard. It left me a little bloody and months later, I still bear a shallow, broad scar across my front.

Seth and I continued digging and exposed the edge of a horn and at that point, I figured the entire animal might be present. So, I decided to call someone with experience for advice or to come out and help. We covered the bones back with dirt and staked a tarp over it. The next weekend Geoff and I returned and uncovered much of the pelvic area, but fearing further damage and acknowledging our lack of expertise, we soon covered it back up.

In the meantime, I sought advice online. I had trouble finding someone willing to make a site visit, but Professor Tom Lehman of Texas Tech University, members of the Austin Paleontological Society, and particularly Joe Taylor, curator of the Mount Blanco Fossil Museum in Crosbyton, Texas, were eager to help me with advice. Joe was interested in the find and was very generous in supporting my endeavor. We corresponded and he mailed me a package that included bison diagrams, including extinct species, as well as a bone-hardening chemical agent that proved to be invaluable to the excavation. This was a package of PVC crystals that when mixed with acetone made a translucent glue that dripped easily and then seeped into the pores and crevices of the bones.

The Austin Paleontological Society put me in touch with a retired University of Texas professor named Dr. Ernest Lundelius at the Vertebrate Paleontology Laboratory on the J.J. Pickle Research campus. Ernie is a great source of knowledge and was able to answer many of my questions. He is retired and was 88 years old at the time, and still spending time in the lab. He thought the species might be the extinct *Bison occidentalis* or possibly a transitional species but could not confirm these thoughts based on photos.

I was still trying to get someone to visit the site to determine if it would be a worthwhile pursuit to excavate when online research led me to David Calame, then a Steward for the Texas Historical Commission. David is a self-described "cowboy archaeologist" and remains my friend to this day. He is Texas' answer to Indiana Jones. When I contacted him in late 2013 he expressed interest in the bison. At that time, I knew I had most of the skeleton present but it was still buried. David asked his archaeologist friend Glenn Goode to come and scout the area. Glenn is a prominent archaeologist who has contributed greatly to the prehistoric knowledge of the Lone Star State. When I took him around the site, he showed me that we were right in the middle of a Native American campsite. He pointed out some telltale features with which I was unfamiliar. He recognized signs of human occupation, particularly fire-cracked burned

Figure 6. Initial exposure of the bison ribs. That cedar post (at top) broke Dad's fall

Figure 7. The eye socket of Rockie's face started to appear

Figure 8. Bruce Turner working on the skull

rock—limestone rock used in "earth ovens" that when heated repeatedly by cooking fires fracture in a distinctive way and accumulate in piles. To an uninformed observer, they just look like rocks. I had also found some broken flint pieces and a couple of Archaic projectile points nearby on the ground surface in the last two years. Glenn indicated to David that he thought the bison skeleton was something potentially worthwhile to excavate due to the close proximity of prehistoric artifacts, so I decided to have the site properly and scientifically excavated and to document our findings.

We waited until Spring 2014 to start the dig and in the meantime I focused on research and site preparation.. My brother Tony brought his large excavator and we removed about seven feet of overburden soil. We had to be careful because there were many roots from the trees I had cut, and many roots were growing right through the skeleton. One bad move and the entire thing could have been pulverized. After a tedious dig and final brush clearing with the excavator, we hand-shoveled a staircase on either side of the skeleton, with one ending at the bison's nose and the other staircase ending at the caudal tail bones. Then we secured a hanging scaffold with ropes tied to trees to access the lower parts. The exposed parts of the skeleton were covered with garden fabric and tarps to keep off any rain.

The last weekend of April 2014, David came out with some acquaintances for the first part of the dig. Bruce Turner is another Texas Historical Commission Steward who attended and we remain friends. Bruce is one of the most knowledgeable people I know when it comes to fossils and artifacts, and I often pester him when I find unusual rocks that I think might be something interesting. David's friend Belinda also stayed at the ranch for the weekend and we excavated the skull. The next weekend we exhumed the rest of the skeleton. As we progressed, I learned about proper archaeological excavating and documenting. We took measurements, screened the surrounding matrix soil, bagged the bones, and labeled everything on a Unique Identity (UI) tracking form. In the screen, we found a few pieces of flint that when later put together looked like puzzle pieces of a shattered arrowhead. When pieced together it appeared to be a Perdiz arrow point—believed to date between 1350-1700 A.D.—consistent with the radiocarbon date later obtained for the skeleton.

We all paused for a while to admire the eye socket when it was first exposed. The last time it had seen the sun was sometime during the prehistory of this continent and the Medieval times of the Old World. There were no cows, horses, wild hogs, or fences on her range. How she stayed in this spot without being washed away was a wonderful mystery.

It took us four full days to finish the job. At night we ate good food, sat in the hot tub, practiced flintknapping, told tall tales, and enjoyed music and cervezas by the campfire. Jessica's grandmother, Marietta Mesecke from Temple, Texas came to spend her 95th birthday at the dig site. Many archaeological enthusiasts and professionals stopped by as well as friends, neighbors, and even the Austin newspaper. The kids loved it!

We had a wonderful time and it was intriguing, rewarding, amazing—one of the most enjoyable

Figure 9. David Calame excavating in the skull area.

Figure 10. Looking east across the creek to the excavation area

and fascinating undertakings in which I have ever participated—and I made some new friends. Braving summer heat, winter cold, ants by the millions, snakes, falling logs, stickers, and a hangover, we finally had the beast exhumed and her face once again saw the light of day after 700 years. It was fantastic.

1/8/16

After the excavation, I made an effort to provide any scientific information that might be gleaned from the bison by seeking out interested parties. Several people from different fields of study were interested. I was approached by the National Bison Association and was asked to register the skeleton as a bison herd. This would allow them to conduct DNA tests that they were looking to pursue, particularly because this specimen was prehistoric: from the period right before early European explorer contact led to interbreeding between cattle and the American Bison. They were hoping to extract genetic information to determine differences between prehistoric bison and the genomes of modern day bison, most or all of which are now mixed with cattle DNA to some degree. I ended up registering the first prehistoric bison into the NBA and sent a mandible (lower jaw) to Oklahoma for genome testing, which I was told might take over a year for the lab to be done.

Figure 11. Upper: The skull of Rockie as it was exposed. Lower" L–R: David Calame, Becky Risor, Ryan Murray

The bones of the skeleton were analyzed by Art Tawater, a faunal specialist and noted North Texas avocational archaeologist (long-time member of the Texas Archeological Society), in December 2014. His findings revealed some rodent gnawing and root etching, but he noted no evidence for any human butchering. He also determined that the animal was a female aged approximately seven years at time of death.

Dr. Barbara Winsborough, from Winsborough Consulting, processed the modern material from the site in the sediment associated with the skull for diatom taxonomy and ecology paleoenvironmental reconstruction. She found a thriving modern assemblage of diatoms in the living collections but nothing remarkable in the surrounding soil.

I also had several volunteers from an online microfossil community examine the interior and exterior cranial matrix soil. I mailed soil samples taken from inside the nasal, oral, and cranial cavities of the skull to several people across the US but no remarkable results were returned.

Dr. Raymond Mauldin at Center for Archaeological Research, The University of Texas at San Antonio, facilitated radiocarbon determination. The analysis showed a 95% probability that the bison lived sometime between 1301 to 1406 A.D. The median calendar date is 1347 A.D.

Figure 12. View across the skeleton during excavation

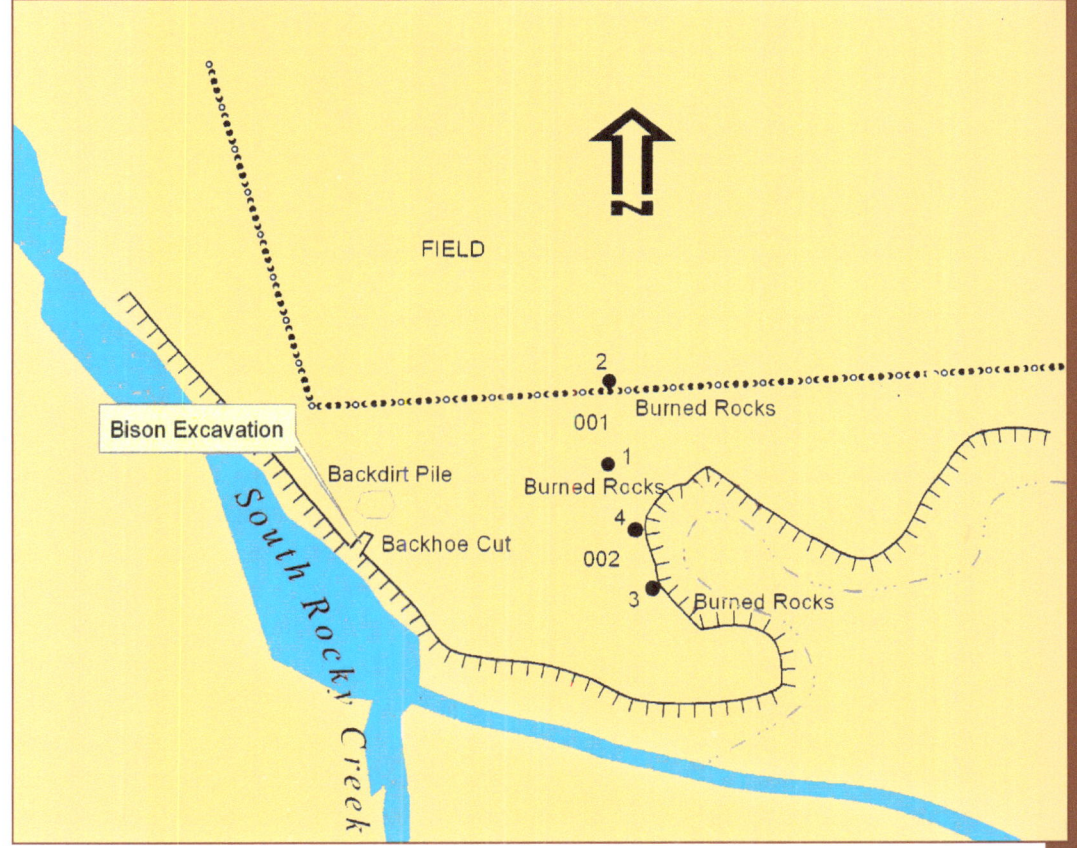

Fig. 13. Site map showing shovel test locations, the Rockie excavation and South Rocky Creek

Figure 14. Vertebral column exposed.

During our work, Chuck Hixson and some members of the Llano Uplift Archeological Society dug four shovel tests to delimit the site area. The locations of the shovel tests (1-4) and the area of the Rockie excavation are shown in the map (see Figure 13).

I still had possession of the skull but had great difficulty keeping it intact, and I sought help online again. I had been applying Joe Taylor's hardening chemicals and was trying to remove some of the matrix soil but could not do it without breaking the bone. Luckily, Ernie invited me to bring the skull to the Vertebrate Paleontology Lab so they could take a look. Their collection of fossils was incredible. I saw a Triceratops skull, a huge pterodactyl wing on the wall, and a basement filled with bones and fossils of all kinds. They also had frogs with translucent skin preserved in jars! You could see their organs through their skin. While I was there, they were opening a field cast of a fossil from the Permian Basin that had encased since the 1930s. When I asked why it had taken so long to unwrap it they said they had a huge backlog of plaster fossils in casts like that. It was a privilege to walk around this place and marvel at what I have heard is the world's fourth largest collection of fossils, as it is

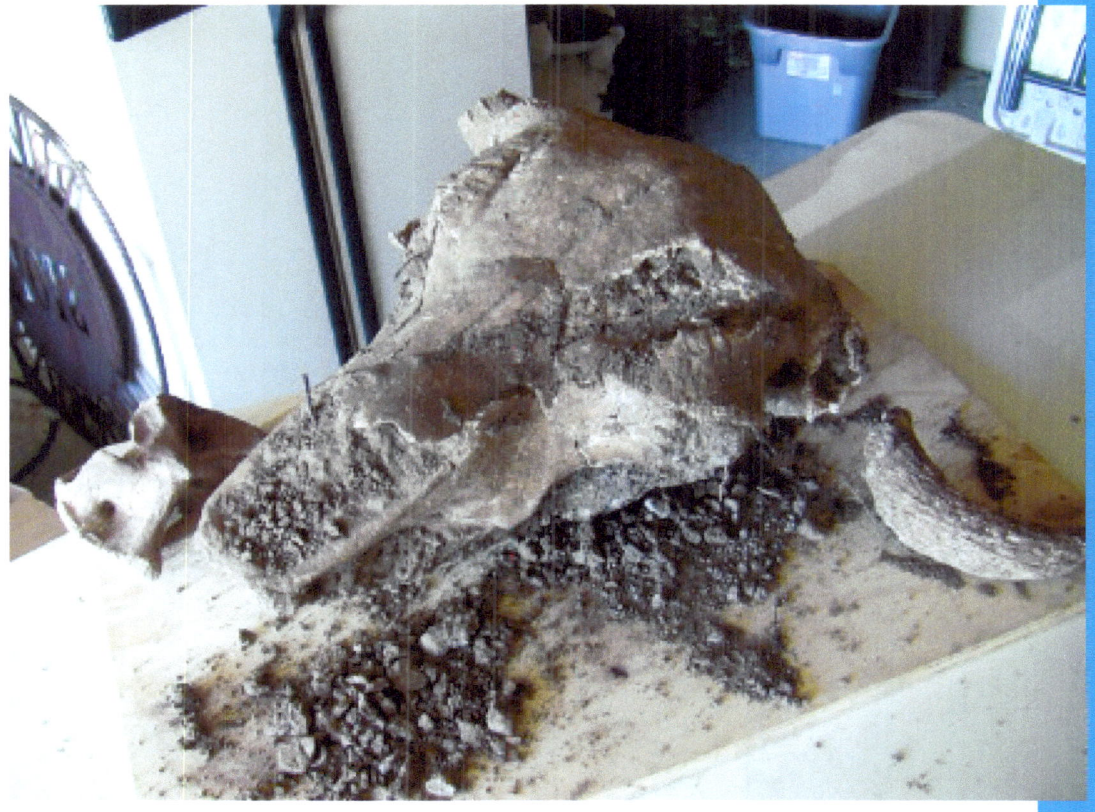

Figure 15. Rockie's skull after excavation and before conservation.

normally closed to the public and only accessible to academics. I am grateful for Ernie's kind invitation. We compared their collection of bison bones with my specimen and they showed me how to apply the hardening agent with more precision. Dr. Lundelius and the lab staff were very generous in their time and were instrumental in showing me how to preserve the skeleton.

4/10/17

In the last year, some of the bones have been traveling the United States for research. The mandible was sent to the North American Bison Registry Chair, Dr. Gerald Parsons in Stratford, Oklahoma, who sent it to a university in California for DNA testing. They were unsuccessful so it was sent to another school and it turned out that the enamel on the teeth was too mineralized for them to extract any DNA so I finally got the mandible back after almost a year and a half.

Jeff Martin was at that time a Ph.D. student at the University of Maine who was doing some research for the bison industry by studying the calcaneum bones and comparing them to determine rates of bison adaptation to rapid climate change. I sent him the only calcaneum that I had and he analyzed it and returned it to me. He presented the results in "Project Bison", a stakeholder science project with bison producers (see Martin's article in this volume).

Arrangements were made to take the bison skeleton to The Falls on the Colorado Museum. I also want to mention the support by Darlene Oostermeyer and Dr. Thomas R. Hester (both on the Board) for their encouragement. I am beyond excited for it to go on display at this wonderful museum in Marble Falls.

Figure 16. Ken Bader assembling the preserved bones as part of exhibit preparation.

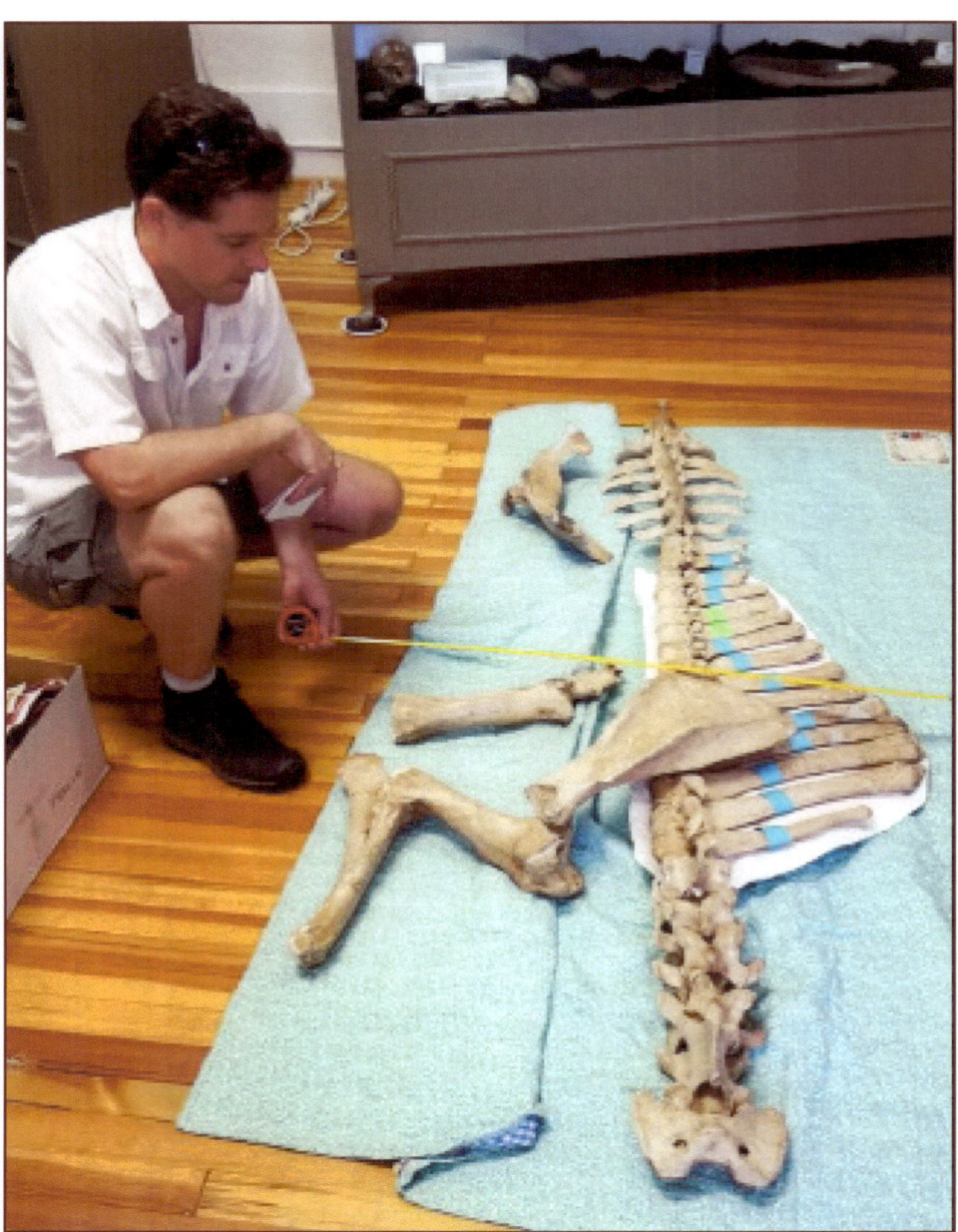

5/20/23

After moving Rockie to The Falls on the Colorado Museum, a preparator named Kenneth Bader (who worked at the UT Vertebrate Paleontology Lab and was recommended by Ernie) expertly took on the project of restoring the skeleton and the painstaking process of piecing the skull back together. During this time he mentioned observing possible cut marks on the radius, ulna, and acetabulum on one of the ilia. Ken did an amazing job conserving and restoring the bones.

Kenneth McBride, a Marble Falls master craftsman, made two exquisite wood and glass display cases. His work at the museum adds so much beauty to many of the exhibits there. I never could have imagined such a great display. *for exhibit.*

Figure 17. Ken McBride with his first smaller case, containing Rockie's skull.

Figure 18. Jane Gelineau standing by Ken McBride's larger case, with Rockie installed for exhibit.

It has been 10 years since I stumbled onto a little piece of bone in a creek and poked around at it. Unraveling her story has been a fascinating journey that has opened doors for me to many more experiences with Texas antiquity. The entire process has led me to a new group of friends and likeminded enthusiasts of fossils and Native American artifacts. I have had the pleasure of

Figure 19. A pencil illustration by Becky Risor titled "The Reveal" depicting the cranium and horns of Rockie.

attending shows with displays at the Oakalla Old Home Days, Legends of the Falls in Cottonwood Shores, and other events to talk about fossils and artifacts. I have joined David Calame at other prehistoric sites including a wooly mammoth skull excavation. Oftentimes I see someone's name like Calame, Goode, and Dr. Thomas R. Hester in the reference notes of books that I read and have to smile. These connections have recently led me to the position of editor and publisher of Texas Cache, a legacy magazine highlighting artifacts from the Lone Star State.

    Throughout the early time when we started scratching around the bones I often wondered, "Is this worth the time and effort?" I now know unequivocally that yes it was. Her place at the museum is an affirmation that the efforts of many people who decided to help get her out of the dirt and eventually to Marble Falls was worth the endeavor. Sadly, Joe Taylor, Becky Risor, and Ken McBride have passed away in the time since, but their contributions to the display live on. A few months after the excavation, Becky mailed me a package and I was pleasantly stunned to see a colored pencil drawing she had made of

Figure 20. David Calame, Ryan Murray, and Bruce Turner at the opening of the Rockie exhibit at The Falls on the Colorado Museum

the skull titled "The Reveal" based on her view during the excavation. I have it hanging in my living room.

When Rockie ended up in her creekside grave, her story did not end then and there. How exactly she met her demise at that spot is unknown. Due to the orientation of her skeleton, it is possible she was stuck in the mud. I have seen cows and hogs stuck in similar positions on collapsed banks. Maybe she died nearby and rode the water current coming to a stop there. Was the broken flint in the dirt from her midsection from a Perdiz arrow point that took her down? Or, had she been shot with the arrow, lived with it inside her body and died some other way? Did the hunters butcher her? There are still many questions but we did get many answers from Rockie.

This project was accomplished through the hard work of a number of people who helped with the excavations and other field tasks. These folks are:

David Calame (foreman),
Bruce Turner,
Becky Risor,
Seth Baldwin,
Todd Johnson,
Geoff "Grizz" Johnson,
Tony Murray,
Jessica Murray,
Ryan Murray,
Duane Murray
and Belinda Cole

I wish to thank the town of Marble Falls, The Falls on the Colorado Museum Board and everyone who donated money and effort to give Rockie a permanent home. I hope she inspires people to appreciate the (pre)history right under our feet. Sometimes the Earth swallows something for a while and then coughs it back out. In this case, that time frame was about 700 years. You just have to watch your step so you don't miss it!

ROCKIE: A LATE PREHISTORIC BISON KILL IN BURNET COUNTY, TEXAS

David L. Calame, Sr., Ryan Murray and Raymond Mauldin

THE SITE AND ENVIRONS

After discovery of the bison remains, detailed in the paper by Murray (this volume), we obtained, from the Texas Archeological Research Laboratory, a trinomial site designation of 41BT506 [41=Texas, BT=Burnet County, 506= this 506th recorded site in the county]. While this designation applies to the area in which Rockie was found, it also includes a small open campsite where time-diagnostic Late Archaic artifacts were collected from the surface. However, the bison skeleton is unrelated to the Late Archaic use of the area. No Late Prehistoric artifacts have been surface collected from 41BT506. The indications, however, of a Late Prehistoric date for the bison skeleton includes a radiocarbon date, and what is almost certainly a badly fractured Perdiz point was

Figure 1. The location of Burnet County in Texas.

found inside the bison's forward body cavity. This find is discussed in greater detail below.

Site 41BT506 is located on the north bank of Little Rocky Creek, also known as Campbells Branch, at its confluence with the South Rocky Creek. The setting is squarely in the middle of central Texas in a transitional zone between the Edwards Plateau and the Blackland Prairie.

EXCAVATION METHODS

The excavation of Rockie was an all-volunteer effort, and with the time constraints and the perilous situation in which we found the bison remains (with regard to possible, future flooding), we decided that the use of a typical archaeological grid would be time-consuming and would not be practical. Instead, the site was carefully mapped, with the skeletal remains clearly plotted. All documentation and measurements were based on scaled recording and photography. In addition to time and other constraints, excavators worked off a scaffold (Figure 2) hung from tree limbs along the creek bank eight feet above the creek (that was four feet deep at the time.)

Figure 2– The senior author excavating the bison, using a scaffold hanging over South Rocky Creek.

Generally, only one excavator could work on the scaffolding at a time and usually worked in direct sunlight. We used small containers (taping and floating pans) to collect excavated soil to be screened. This allowed for the screening to keep pace with the excavation. With immediate notification from screening volunteers, any artifacts not found in place could then be pinpointed near its original position in the excavation. As it turned out this precaution was critical to the excavation's success.

Excavators wore surgical gloves while excavating and handling the bison bones, and generally used a short Phillips-head screwdriver sharpened to a point. This tool provided excavators great control when working close to, and in between, bones. Metal pointing trowels were used in open areas in which we knew there was no bone. Every attempt was made not to scar the bones with metal tools.

The overburden, which contained no archaeological material, was removed with a large track excavator and a staging platform created, the scaffolding was created. Then, the scaffolding was set in place.

The excavations first concentrated on uncovering and preserving the bison skull. Once that was accomplished, the exact position of the bison's body was determined and all overburden to within 12 inches over the body was removed gently with shovels, cutting back approximately 36 inches into the bank.

Excavators followed individual bones, referring often to a printed bison skeleton handout, to identify the skeletal elements. As bones were excavated and recorded, they were removed, closely examined, then bagged, tagged and packed away safely. Once the ribs on the right (upper) site had been removed, soil in the body cavity was excavated approximately two quarts in volume at a time and immediately screened and saved as soil samples. It was during this process that the tiny fractured Perdiz arrow point was discovered and recovered in four pieces. Because of the small quantities of soil being removed and screened, it was possible to place the fractured arrow point in the area behind the third and fourth rib from the animal's front and in a mid-cage position.

After excavations were completed, it was determined the entire animal was present, with the exception of the lower leg sections, including the hooves. It is assumed these missing parts had previously been eroded into the creek before the bison discovery.

EXAMINING THE ARROW POINT

During the fieldwork, the senior author felt that any stone artifacts that might be found would be of a Late Prehistoric affiliation. Having observed shattered arrow points from previously excavated bison kill sites, we knew it is difficult to recognize them as anything other than small flint flakes (Cindy Smyers, personal communication). As the pieces were fitted the length, minus the missing stem, is 17 mm, and the width, approximately 13 mm.

Close examination of this artifact determined that it exhibited an original flake surface on one side, meaning that it is a unifacially flaked projectile point.

> *Excavators wore surgical gloves while excavating and handling the bison bones*

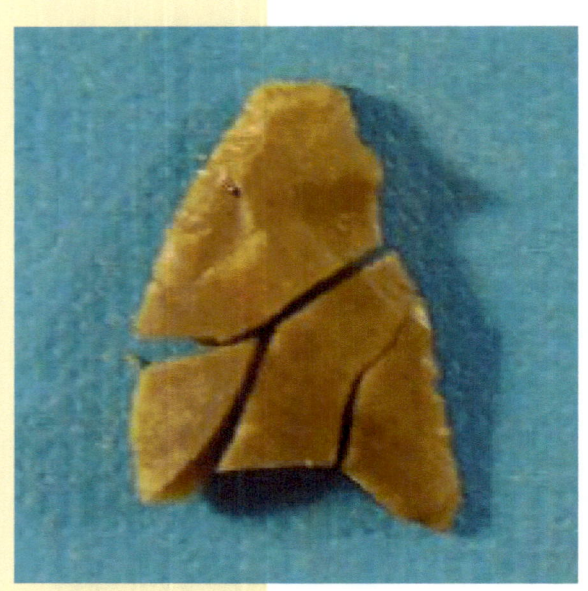

Figure 3. The Perdiz arrowpoint re-assembled from flint fragments found in the front rib cage of the bison. The stem is missing. Length is 17 mm, width, 13 mm.

The flint (chert) of which this fractured point is made is light grayish brown in color and of a very high quality. The material fluoresced pumpkin orange under an ultraviolet (UV) light in both short and long wave using a Mineral Lamp Model UVGL-55 Multiband UV- 254/365 NM. Based on research on the UV analysis of Texas cherts (Hofman et al. 1991), the pumpkin orange color indicates it is made of Edwards Plateau chert.

Based on the traits of the point, which would have included a contracted, pointed stem, and along with an intact pointed barb, we feel strongly that the specimen is of the Perdiz type (Turner et al. 2011:206). This type is a hallmark of the Toyah Phase, ca. 1300-1700 A.D. The Toyah Phase is well documented as bison-hunting peoples in central Texas and adjacent parts of the state

RADIOCARBON DATING

Dating of the Burnet bison sample followed an acid-base-acid protocol for collagen (see Brock et al., 2010, Longin 1971; Minami et al. 2004). The surface of the bone sample was initially removed with a rotary tool. The sample was then cut out and lightly crushed in a ceramic mortar and pestle to create fragments, roughly 0.5 to 2.0 mm in size. These were next repeatedly sonicated in ultra-pure water, with water changed after each 60-minute period. When the water was clear following a run, samples were then dried under low heat. Two 150 mg samples of bone were then weighed into glass test tubes. These were decalcified by the addition of 0.5 N hydrochloric acid (HCL) and maintained at 4°C for 30 hours. The two samples were next washed to neutral in ultra-pure water. They were then treated with 0.1 N sodium hydroxide (NaOH) for 30 to 45 minutes at room temperature. After washing again to neutral, the two samples were combined and refrigerated for 18 hours in 0.5 N HCL. The 0.5 N HCL was replaced with 0.01 HCL and heated in a dry bath at 70°C to place the collagen into solution. When complete, the solution was filtered through a 0.45-micron silver filter into a glass vial.

The sample was frozen and, after freeze drying, shipped to DirectAMS (Zoppi et al. 2007) for analysis. At DirectAMS the pre-treated collagen was combusted, reduced to graphite, and measured by accelerator mass spectrometry (AMS; see Zoppi et al. 2007). The sample returned a date of 603 +/- 27 Radiocarbon Years Before Present (RCYBP; D-AMS 11290; percent modern carbon 92.77% with a measured $\delta 13 C$ of -5.2‰). When calibrated using the OxCal (version 4.4) radiocarbon calibration program (Bronk Ramsey 2009) and the IntCal 20 calibration curve, the sample returned a date of 1301 to 1406 cal AD at 95.4% probability, a distribution with a median date of 1347 cal AD (Figure 1). The most likely date range for the Burnet bison, with a 72.4% probability, is between AD 1301 and 1370.

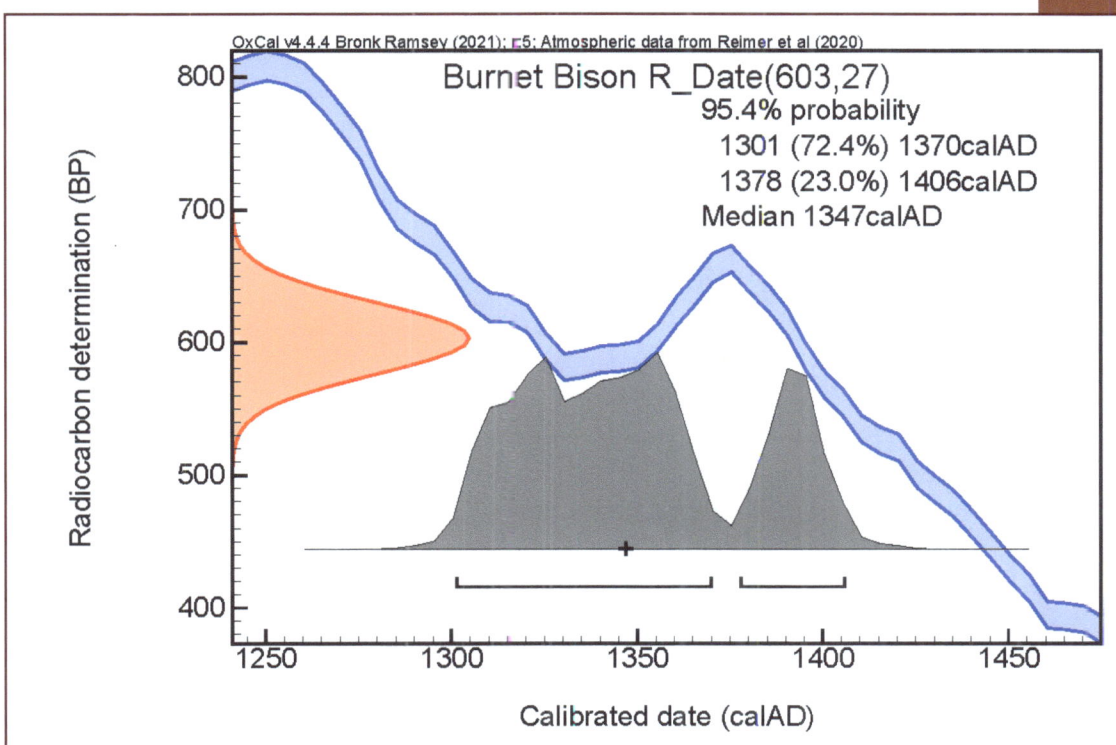

Figure 4 Calibration results for the Burnet Bison. The orange curve shows the measured date of 603 RCYBP, with a standard deviation of 27. The blue line is the 2020 calibration, with the gray probability curve showing the intersection of the measured sample with the calibration curve. The + identifies the location of the median date, with the underlying bars showing the range at 95.4% probability.

DISCUSSION

Since this bison was almost completely intact, had it been butchered in any way? Art Tawater, who did the faunal analysis found no butchering marks on the bones. However, Ken Bader, the vertebrate paleontologist who cleaned and conserved the skeleton, observed marks from what could be butchering or rodent gnawing. The marks were recorded on photographs by Bader. He notes the marks are present only on condyles where the adjacent bones are missing. This suggests, in his view, that these are places where butchering marks might be found (Ken Bader, personal communication with Thomas R. Hester, July 27, 2023).

However, since the Perdiz point was found within the bison's body cavity, it is almost certainly the cause of its demise. The likely scenario seems that the animal escaped an attack badly wounded, only to die later from this wound. Whatever the case, the bison's body was quickly covered in silt, preventing scavengers from scattering the bones.

Considering the excavated data, the remains of Rockie should be regarded as a "bison kill," but with the details remaining largely unknown.

ACKNOWLEDGMENTS

We thank the property owners, Mr. and Mrs. Duane Murray and Mr. and Mrs. Ryan Murray, for allowing the excavation on their property. Not only were they all very active in the excavation itself, but they also provided room and board to all the volunteers and from a logistical standpoint made this excavation not only possible but very enjoyable.

Next, thanks to The University of Texas at San Antonio's Center for Archaeological Research and Dr. Raymond Mauldin for the radiocarbon dating of these bison remains. Thanks as well to Art Tawater for his expertise in examining these bones for possible butchery marks. We thank Dr. Thomas R. Hester, both for editing this publication —and as an advisor who took time to consider facts and give his thoughts. We also appreciate the input of Dr. Ernest Lundelius of the Vertebrate Paleontology Laboratory at The University of Texas at Austin and Joe Taylor of Crosbyton, Texas,

Finally, great thanks are offered to all the volunteers as listed in Ryan Murray's article (this volume.) We would add our appreciation to Glenn Goode for coming to the site and offering his advice, and to the awesome crew cook, Kathy Murray

REFERENCES CITED

Brock, F., T. Higham, P. Ditchfield, and C. Bronk Ramsey
2010 Current Pre-treatment Methods for AMS Radiocarbon Dating at the Oxford Radiocarbon Accelerator Unit (ORAU). *Radiocarbon* 52: 103-112.

Bronk Ramsey, C.
2009 Bayesian Analysis of Radiocarbon Rates. *Radiocarbon* 51: 337-360.

Hofman, J. L. L. C. Todd and M. B. Collins
1991 Identification of Central Texas Chert at the Folsom and Lindenmeier Sites. *Plains Anthropologist* 36 (131):297-308.

Longin, R.
1971 New Model of Collagen Extraction for Radiocarbon Dating. *Nature* 230: 241-242.

Turner, E. S., T. R. Hester, and R. L. McReynolds
2011 *Stone Artifacts of Texas Indians*. 3rd revised edition, Taylor Trade Publishing, Rowman and Littlefield, Lanham, Maryland

Zoppi, U., Crye, J., Song, Q.
2007 Performance Evaluation of the New AMS System at Accium BioSciences. *Radiocarbon* 49, 171-180.

> *... likely scenario seems that the animal escaped an attack badly wounded, only to die later from this wound.*

BODY SIZE OF THE ROCKY CREEK SITE BISON, BURNET COUNTY, TEXAS, USA: CONTEXT AND EXPLANATIONS

Jeff M. Martin

Background

In ecology and biology, body mass is a useful measure to predict dietary requirements, metabolic energy budgets, among other biological functions (Martin et al., 2018). Much of my research is focused on body size reconstructions and the consequences of body size change in response to global climate change. In a warming world, smaller body sizes will dominate. Body sizes are largely a plastic character that provides insight to ecological processes at play. These changes have profound effects on populations in production systems and nutrient cycling in ecological systems. Bison today express a 30% body mass gradient from north to south, that is, Bison in Saskatchewan (52°N) are at least 30% larger than those in Texas (30°N (Craine 2013)). This body size gradient is likely associated with latitudinal variation in timing of reproduction and parturition as well as windows for growth (Barboza et al., 2009). Bison provide an excellent resource to test and understand thermal relationships with body mass across space and through time because of their complete fossil record and wide distribution across large latitudes and diverse ecoregion provinces.

Methods

Linear bone measures of the calcaneum were standard following a few resources (Von Den Driesch 1976; Hill 1996; Hill et al. 2008). A comparative dataset of osteomeasures of Bison sp. calcanea was assembled ($n=849$) and missing values for DstL were replaced by specific linear regression analysis of GL to DstL relationships (Martin et al., 2018; 5). The distal tuber length (DstL) in particular was used to calculate an estimated mass (M) as $M = (DstL/11.49)^3$ following Christiansen (2002). Average annual temperature was estimated from $\delta^{18}O$ values in the ice cores from Greenland following Grootes and colleagues

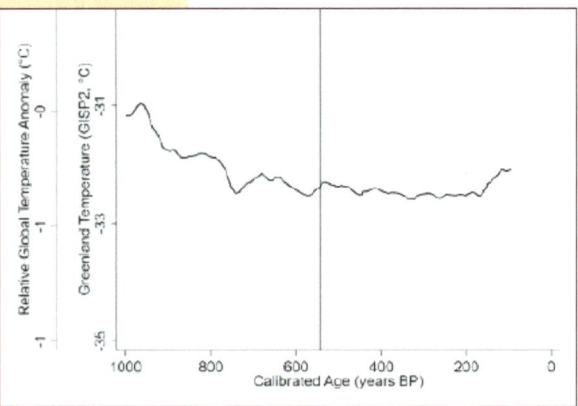

Figure 1. Sequence of Greenland mean annual temperature (°C derived from GISP2 δ¹⁸O values (Grootes et al. 1993; Alley 2000; Alley and Ágústsdóttir 2005)) and relative global temperature anomaly derived from modern Greenland temperatures (29.9°C mean annual temperature, circa CE 2010) from 2,000 years ago (left) to CE 1855 (right). Vertical line indicates the Rocky Creek Site calibrated age (global anomaly at 603 years BP was -0.51°C).

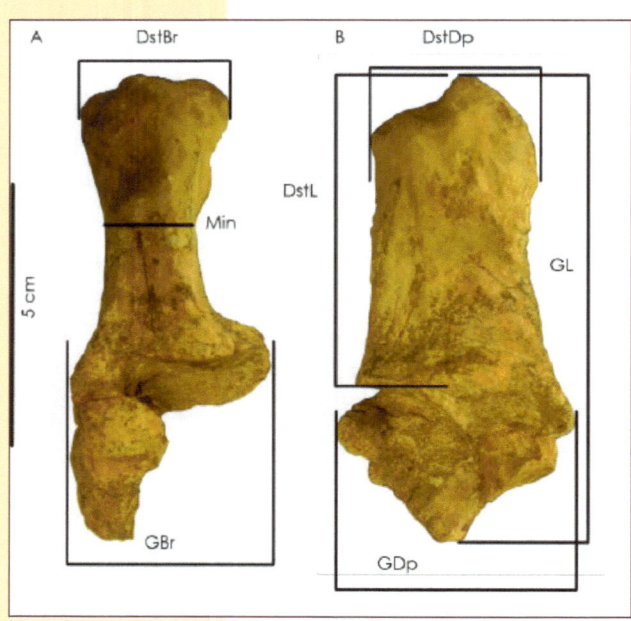

Figure 2. Measurement scheme of the calcaneum. A) Anterior view (from the top), B) medial view (from the anatomical middle looking outwards). Abbreviations: GL; greatest length, GDp; greatest depth of sustentaculum, GBr; greatest breadth of sustentaculum, DstBr; distal breadth of calcaneal tuber, Min; minimum diaphysis width of calcaneal tuber, DstL; distal length of the calcaneal tuber, DstDp; distal depth of the calcaneal tuber (Von Den Driesch 1976; Hill 1996).

(Grootes et al., 1993; Alley, 2000). We used mixed model regressions for each metric of the calcaneum to compare species as a fixed effect with *B. bison* as the base for the comparison (Stata v15.1, 2018, StataCorp, College Station, TX, USA). Similarly, mixed models were used to compare DstL with other calcaneal metrics with species as a fixed effect. All mixed models included site as a random effect to account for repeated measures within each location. We used the robust "sandwich estimator" to relax assumptions of normal distribution and homogeneity of variance for the regression (Bolker et al. 2009; Rabe-Hesketh and Skrondal 2012).

Results

Paleotemperature data, derived from (Grootes et al. 1993; Alley 2000) is presented in Figure 1 of the last 1000 years. The South Rocky Creek bison, at AD 1301-1370 calibrated years BP during the Holocene, was on average 0.51° cooler than modern Anthropocene conditions. Warmer conditions are expected for the 21st century, between 2-4°C warmer than the 20th century average (IPCC Working Group 1, 2014).

Linear measures (Figure 1) of "Rockie" and Bison averages are reported in Table 1. Overall, "Rockie" nearly represents the mean for *Bison spp.* measures. The Rockie Creek site calcaneal measures of GL and DstL are reported with other contemporaneous sites for comparative analysis in Table 2 and presented in Figure 3. Overall, with the contemporaneous sites within 200 years of the Rocky Creek site, "Rockie" represents a slightly above average individual, but still represents an average body mass for all *Bison spp.*

Comparative bi-plots of linear osteometrics are presented in Figures 4 and 5. The DstL is a useful measure because is captures a functional aspect of the calcaneum. It is what directly attaches to the Achilles tendon and is responsible for displacing the force of locomotion and mass of the animal. It has also been found to indicate the traits through the use of ecometrics (Eronen et al. 2010; Polly et al. 2011, 2017). More studies will be conducted using these measures and traits in the future to understand climate change impacts on animal communities. Relating DstL to GBr and GL is useful in understanding the taxonomic relationship of most other taxa, but in Bison specimens, these measures largely overlap, supporting the claim that the included species may all be the same species, a chronospecies, adapting to climate change through time.

Generally, described as Bergmann's Rule (Bergmann 1847), endotherms increase in body size with increasing latitude (Huston and Wolverton 2011). It is likely that negative correlation between temperature and latitude is driving Bergmann's rule (i.e., body size) because even though we found that bison are larger at cooler temperatures, we were unable to correlate a significant effect of latitude over the geologic record ($p > .94$). The negative relationship between body mass and global temperature may reflect underlying relationships between body size and net primary production as well as heat loads (Speakman and Król, 2010; Huston and Wolverton 2011).

Table 1. Summary table of osteometrics of "Rockie" the bison calcaneum from Burnet County, Texas. Parameter abbreviations are detailed in Figure 1. Note, Min is not reported for the species mean because it has been shown to not be a significant measure.

Parameter	Measure (mm)	*Bison* mean
GL	156.55	153.4
DstL	96.96	99.7
GDp	59.98	60.3
GBr	49.42	51.9
DstBr	38.83	40.2
DstDp	41.18	43.2
Min	21.50	—

Table 2. Summary statistics of contemporary bison, within 200 years, to "Rockie" by locality of calcaneal measures of greatest length (GL), distal tuber length (DstL), and estimated body dfmass (M).

Site Name	Calibrated Age (years BP)	GL			DstL			M		
		N	Mean	SD	N	Mean	SD	N	Mean	SD
Garnsey	475	7	148.3	8.1	7	95.9	7.0	7	590.0	134.4
Big Goose	520	16	148.3	7.8	16	96.1	4.9	16	589.4	87.9
Big Bone Lick	535	26	142.5	8.0	28	93.7	5.9	28	548.5	107.4
Rocky Creek	603	1	156.6	—	1	97.0	—	1	601.0	—
Baker Cave	695	23	147.2	6.8	23	95.0	5.8	23	571.1	107.3

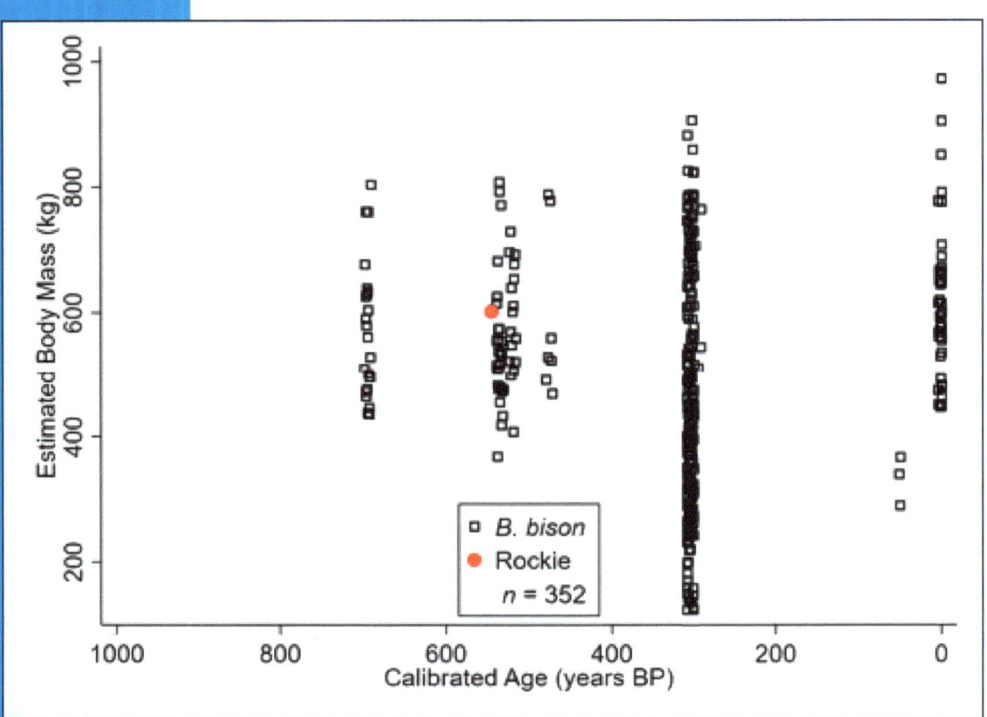

Figure 3. Temporal plot of estimated body mass of Bison cf. B. bison (black hollow squares, data points are "jittered" to illustrate density) over the last 1000 years including "Rockie" (red solid circle).

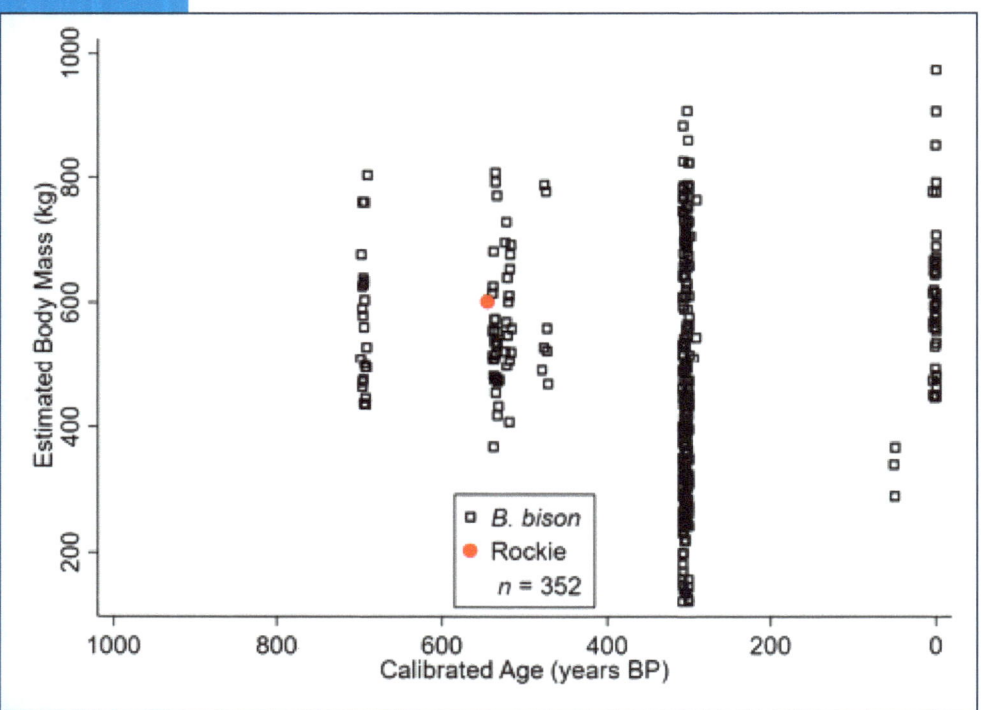

Figure 4. Scatter plot of calcaneal measures greatest breadth (GBr) and distal tuber length (DstL) from 1,011 Bison spp. across North America with "Rockie" indicated in the red solid circle.

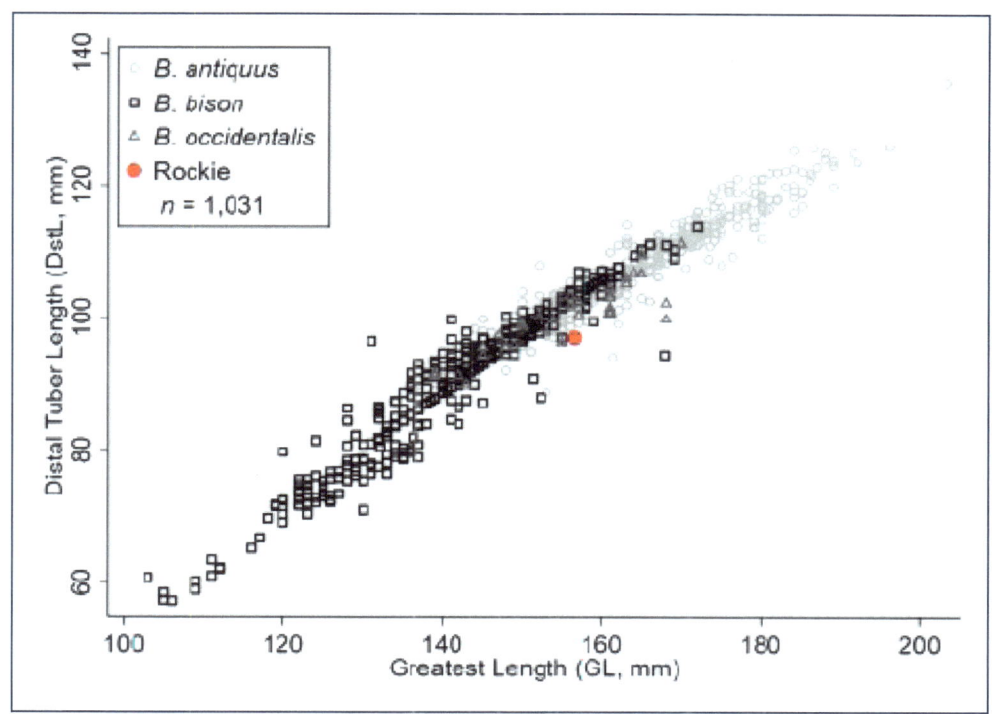

Figure 5. Scatter plot of calcaneal measures greatest length (GL) and distal tuber length (DstL) from 1,031 Bison spp. across North America with "Rockie" indicated in the red solid circle.

The relationship between calcaneal distal tuber length (DstL) and relative global temperature was −1.77 mm/°C ± 0.45 ($z = -3.95$, $p < .001$) with intercepts at 92 ± 2 mm for *B. bison*, 103 ± 3 mm for *B. antiquus*, and 101 ± 2 mm for *B. occidentalis* (Martin et al., 2018). Consequently, the slope of estimated body mass with global temperature was also negative at −41 kg/°C (± 10; $z = -4.10$, $p < .001$) with intercepts at 521 ± 36 kg for *B. bison*, 737 ± 45 kg for *B. antiquus*, and 676 ± 36 kg for *B. occidentalis* (Martin et al., 2018). This relationship predicts that *B. bison* will decrease by 164 ± 40 kg to 357 ± 54 kg if global temperature rises from 0°C to +4°C (Martin et al., 2018). If we ignore species designations and analyze our data at the clade level, the slope of podial size with increasing temperatures becomes steeper; −63 kg/°C (±10; $z = -6.11$ $p < .001$) with an intercept at 648 ± 26 kg for *Bison spp.*, as compared to the −41 kg/°C for *Bison bison* (Figure 6).

Discussion

Rockie provides a look into the evolution and ecology of Bison in the context of changing climates across both space and time. Although a mature animal, Rockie is not as large as some of her northern contemporaries and likely never would have been due to several factors related to growth.

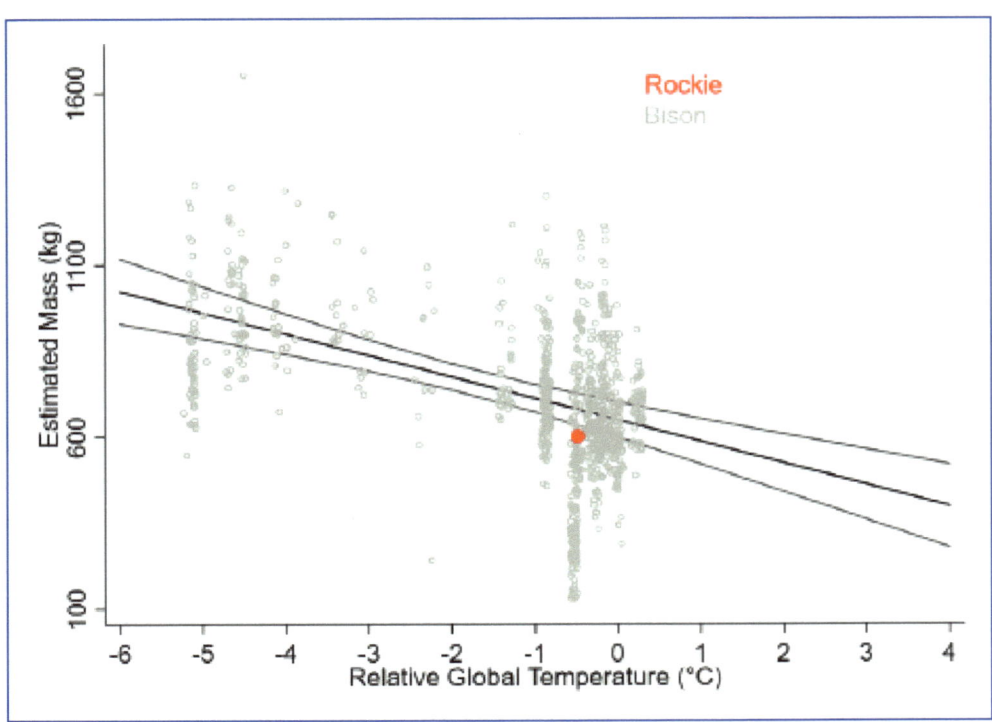

Figure 6. Relationship between estimated Bison body mass (gray hollow circles, data points are "jittered" to illustrate density; kg) and the linear effect of relative global temperature (°C derived from GISP2 ^{18}O values (Grootes et al., 1993)) from the mixed model regression with fixed effects of temperature and the random effect of site. Regression line for Bison (black line) is -63 kg/°C (± 10; z = -6.11 p < .001) with an intercept at 648 ± 26 kg with "Rockie" indicated in the red solid circle (modified from Martin et al., 2018).

Several authors have indicated that *Bison antiquus*, *B. occidentalis*, and *B. bison* (and some also argue *Bison priscus* and *B. latifrons*) are all the same species adapting to extreme environmental change through time (Valerius Geist, 1991; Shapiro et al., 2004; Wilson et al., 2008; Zazula et al., 2017; Martin et al., 2018). Quantifying and comparing physiological thresholds and mechanisms driving body size change are imperative for managing Bison and other large herbivores. Conservation goals among latitudinally disparate Bison herds in North America should consider that resident Bison will likely grow smaller and more slowly in the south than in the north, which will impact management strategies at both regional and continental scales.

REFERENCES CITED

Alley, R.B
2000 The Younger Dryas cold interval as viewed from central Greenland. *Quaternary Science Reviews* 19:213-226.

Alley,R.B., and A. M. Ágústsdóttir
2005 The 8k event: Cause and consequences of a major Holocene abrupt climate change. *Quaternary Science Reviews* 24:1123-1149.

Barboza, P.S, K. L. Parker and I. D. Hume
2009 *Integrative Wildlife Nutrition*. Springer, Heidelberg, Germany, 350 pp.

Bergmann, C.
1847 *Ueber die Verhältnisse der wärmeökonomie der Thiere zu ihrer Grösse*. Gottinger Studien 3(1):596-707. Gottingen, Germamy.

Bolker, B.M., M. E. Brooks, C, J. Clark, S. W. Geange, J. R. Poulsen. H. M. H. Stevens, and J. S. S. White
2009 Generalized linear mixed models: a practical guide for ecology and evolution. *Trends in Ecology and Evolution* 24: 127-135.

Christiansen, P.
2002 Locomotion in terrestrial mammals: The influence of body mass, limb length and bone proportions on speed. *Zoological Journal of the Linnean Society* 136:685-714.

Craine, J.M.
2013 Long-term climate sensitivity of grazer performance: a cross-site study. *PLOS ONE*, https://dot,org/10.1271/journal pone.00067065.

Von Den Driesch, A.
1976 *A guide to the measurement of animal bones from archeological sites*, 1st ed.. Peabody Museum, Harvard University, Harvard, Massachusetts.

Eronen, J.T., P. D. Polly, M. Fred et al.
2010 Ecometrics: The traits that bind the past and present together. *Integrative Zoology* 5:88-101.

Grootes, P,. M. Stuiver, J. White, S. Johnsen and J. Jouzel
1993 Comparison of oxygen isotope records from the GISP2 and GRIP Greenland ice cores. *Nature* 366.

Hill, M. G,
1996 Size comparison of the Mill Iron Site bison calcanea. In: *The Mill Iron Site* ed. by G. C. Frison, pp. 231-237. University of New Mexico Press, Albuquerque, New Mexico.

Hill, M.E.,M. G. Hill and C. C. Widga
2008 Late Quaternary Bison diminution on the Great Plains of North America: Evaluating the role of human hunting versus climate change. *Quaternary Science Reviews* 27:1752-1771.

Huston, M. A. and S. Wolverton \
2011 Regulation of animal size by eNPP, Bergmann's rule, and related phenomena. *Ecological Monographs* 81:349-405.

IPCC Working Group 1
2014 IPCC Fifth Assessment Report (AR5) – The physical science basis. *IPCC*.

Martin. J. M,.,J. I. Mead and P. S. Barboza
2018 Bison body size and climate change. *Ecology and Evolution* 8:4564-4574.

Polly P.D., J. T. Eronen, M. Fred et al.
2011 History matters: ecometrics and integrative climate change biology. *Proceedings. Biological sciences / The Royal Society* 278: 1131-40.

Polly. P.D., J. Fuentes-Gonzalez, A,M. Lawing. A. K. Bormet AK, and R. G. Dundas
2017 Clade sorting has a greater effect than local adaptation on ecometric patterns in Carnivora. *Evolutionary Ecology Research* 18:61-95.

Rabe-Hesketh, S. and A. Skrondal
2012 *Multilevel and longitudinal modeling using*

Stata, Third edition. Stata Press, College Station, Texas.

Shapiro, B, A. J. Drummond,, A .Rambaut et al.
2004 Rise and fall of the Beringian steppe bison. *Science* 306: 1561–1565.

Speakman J.R., and E.Król
2010 Maximal heat dissipation capacity and hyperthermia risk: neglected key factors in the ecology of endotherms. *Journal of Animal Ecology* 79; 726–746.

Valerius, G.
1991 Phantom subspecies: The wood bison *Bison bison* "athabascae" Rhoads 1897 is not a valid taxon, but an ecotype. *Arctic* 44: 283–300.

Wilson M.C., L. V.Hills, and B. Shapiro
2008 Late Pleistocene northward-dispersing Bison antiquus from the Bighill Creek Formation, Gallelli Gravel Pit, Alberta, Canada, and the fate of Bison occidentalis. *Canadian Journal of Earth Sciences* 45: 827–859.

Zazula, G,D., E. Hall, P. G. Hare, et al.
2107 A middle holocene steppe bison and paleoenvironments from the versleuce meadows, Whitehorse, Yukon, Canada. *Canadian Journal of Earth Sciences* 54:1138–1152.

ROCKIE'S PREPARATION

Kenneth Bader

When Rockie's bones arrived at the museum, most were not intact. Years of shrinking and swelling of the clays in the surrounding soil fractured the bones, and the skeleton was collected in chunks and stored in plastic bags. The first step was to clean all of the soil from the bones. Luckily, most of the bone fragments were well-preserved and the soil quickly softened in water. Then, each fragment was briefly submerged and scrubbed with a toothbrush. Thick clay was removed using a bamboo skewer, which was less likely to scratch the bone than a metal tool. The clean bones were laid out on newspaper for a few days to dry. After the bone fragments dried, thin B-72 was brushed over the surface. B-72 is a thermoplastic resin that can be dissolved in acetone or denatured alcohol to a desired consistency (Figure 1). Evaporation of the solvent leaves the B-72 behind. A thin, watery

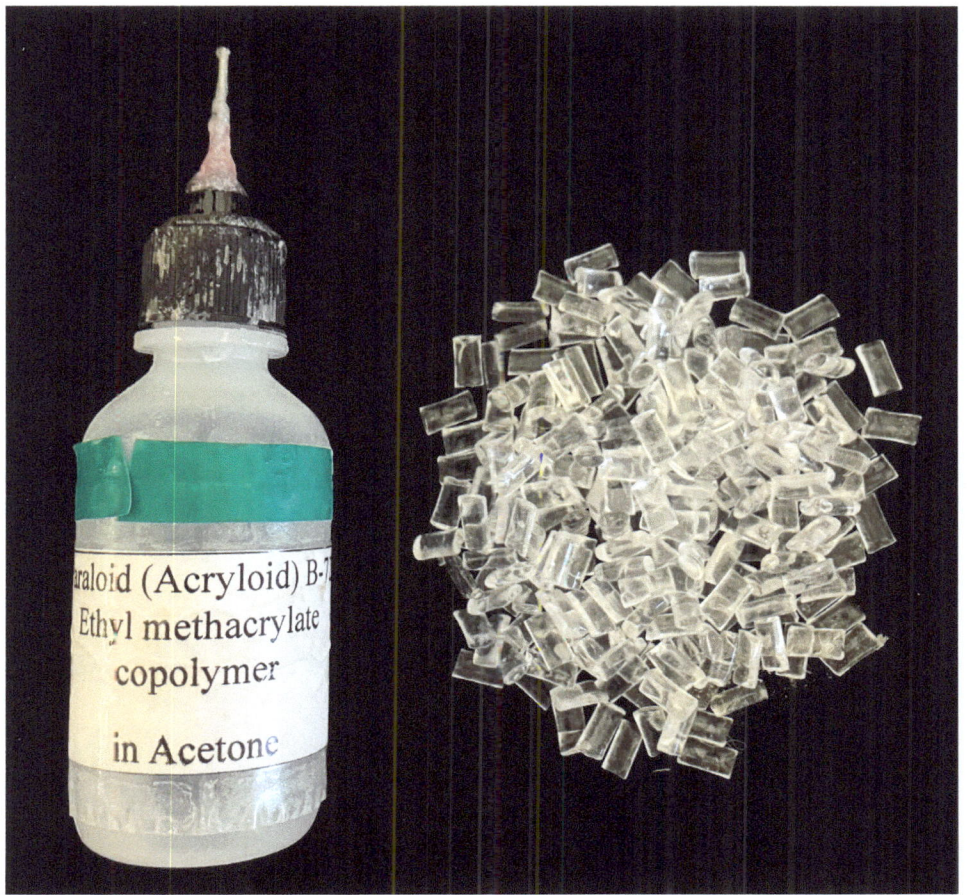

Figure 1. Solid plastic beads of Paraloid B-72 are soluble in acetone and provide a reversible alternative to super glue.

mix of B-72 soaks into the pore spaces of the bone and acts a hardener. Thick B-72 can be used to glue bone fragments together. B-72 and similar adhesives are preferred over superglues in paleontology and archaeology because it can be reversed by reapplication of the solvent.

It took four months to sort through the ~1,000 bone fragments to reassemble Rockie's vertebrae, ribs, pelvis, scapulae, and limb bones. When bone fragments were found that fit back together, thick B-72 was brushed onto the contact surface and the bones were set upright in a small sandbox until the adhesive cured. Some portions of the bones were missing, either due to weathering or because they were lost during excavation. When necessary for structural support, these gaps with filled with epoxy putty. The putty is gray in color and can be easily distinguished from the natural bone. I decided against painting the putty so that researchers and the public could easily identify the reconstructed areas. The fragile nature of the bones and absence of most of the limb bones prevented us from mounting Rockie in a standing position. Such a mount would have required extensive metalwork and the skeleton would have been vulnerable to vibrations. We decided instead to lay the skeleton out in the position that it was found and recreate the excavation setting (Figure 2).

In this position, each bone would be fully supported in either a plaster cradle or on sand and could be removed easily for research. The original dirt could be replicated with garnet abrasive, a sand-blasting medium that produces very little dust.

The carcass of a three-year-old male bison, minus the head, was obtained from a local rancher to fill in for some of the missing bones in Rockie's skeleton. The flesh was removed from the bones using a technique called maceration. The carcass was allowed to rot in buckets of water until the muscles liquified and only the bones and hooves were left. Unfortunately, after the bones were clean and disinfected, we discovered that Rockie was considerably larger than its modern counterpart. We decided to display these bones in a secondary exhibit case alongside bones from Rockie's left side.

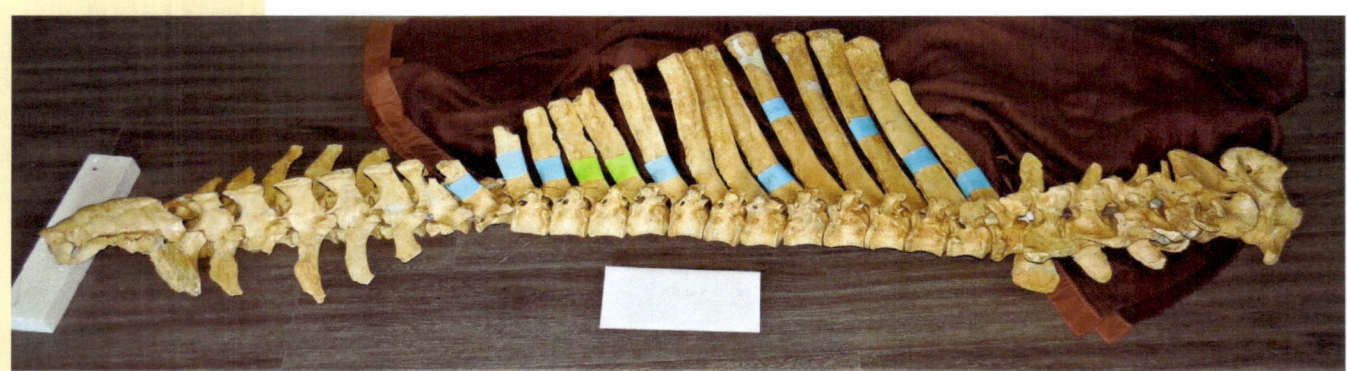

Figure 2. Rockie's vertebral column laid out and ready for construction of the plaster support cradles.

The skull arrived mostly in one piece with the articulated right lower jaw. The outer surfaces were previously cleaned for temporary exhibition and a clear adhesive was applied to the skull, trapping some soil on the bone surface. The glue was softened with acetone and slowly peeled off with bamboo skewers. Once the surface was clean, it was hardened with a thin coat of B-72. The skull has a rough texture and was never scrubbed clean with water, resulting in a slightly different finished color than the bones in the rest of the skeleton. The lower jaw needed to be removed to provide access to the underside of the skull for cleaning. A plaster jacket was constructed for the right side of the face and lower jaw with a layer of plastic wrap placed over the bone surface to protect it. Modeling clay was used to fill holes and undercuts. Burlap strips were dipped into a 2:1 mixture of plaster and water and placed over the plastic wrap. The resulting jacket uniformly supported the bones and prevented breakage when the skull was rolled onto its right side. The underside of the skull was delicate, with many thin bony projections so an eyedropper was used to add water to soften small patches of soil, which could then be scraped away with bamboo skewers. Soil was left around the most fragile structures, which were stabilized with B-72. When the lower jaw was ready to be removed, a second support jacket was made for the top of the skull so it could safely be turned upside down. The remaining soil was softened, and the jaw was lifted out in one piece. A fracture plane split the left side of the face from the rest of the skull during excavation. After these facial bones were cleaned, they were not reattached because they were too thin and fragile to support the weight of the skull. A third plaster jacket was constructed to support the underside of the skull while it is on display.

Once the bones were fully prepared, photographs from the excavation were used as a guide to lay out the articulated skeleton so that dimensions for the exhibit case could be determined (9 feet long by 4 feet wide). To simplify the installation, plaster cradles were constructed for the articulated vertebral column and ribs (Figure 3). A plaster cradle is a reinforced support jacket with plaster legs that help it sit flat on a table. The burlap is replaced with woven fiberglass cloth, which will not deteriorate in fluctuating humidity or attract insect pests. Due to the length of the vertebral column, I constructed two cradles, one for the thoracic (chest) vertebrae and one for the lumbar vertebrae and sacrum. The completed cradles were lined up and bound together with an extra layer of fiberglass and plaster. The cervical (neck) vertebrae were rested on sand. This provided the flexibility to orient the skull to match photographs of the skeleton as it was found in the ground.

With the thoracic vertebrae resting in their cradle, the first six ribs (which are visible in photographs from the excavation) were positioned and held in place with modeling clay. A support jacket was used to hold the ribs in anatomical position so they could be turned over to make the plaster cradle for the display. The resulting cradle holds the shafts of the ribs in position while the rib head hangs off the cradle to articulate with the thoracic vertebrae in the

> *The skull arrived mostly in one piece with the articulated right lower jaw.*

Figure 3. Installing the plaster support cradles and vertebral column in the exhibit case.

adjacent vertebral cradle. Mounting the right scapula provided an interesting challenge. Scapulae are attached to the outside of the ribcage by tendons and ligaments. Bison lack clavicles, the bones that attach the scapulae to the sternum in humans. The only way to include the right scapula on Rockie's skeleton would be to either add extra sand and bury the ribcage or construct a pedestal that would hold it slightly above the ribcage. In order to show as much of the skeleton as possible, a pedestal was constructed that would be mostly invisible to museum visitors. The pedestal needed to run along the underside of the scapula, include clips to prevent the scapula from sliding off the pedestal, and attach to the cradle for the ribs below. Brass rods were used under the scapula to build the support structure. Then the scapula was placed upside-down in the sand box and the brass rods were embedded into a narrow plaster cradle. The resulting pedestal supported the scapula from underneath and the brass rods held the bone in place. As with all cradles in Rockie's mount, the scapula can be easily lifted off the pedestal. Holes were drilled into the pedestal, and it was attached to underlying the cradle with bolts (Figure 4). A small piece of felt was added underneath the pedestal to help stabilize the pedestal and prevent rubbing against the underlying ribs. The whole pedestal was spray painted black to make it inconspicuous. In October 2018 the exhibit case was ready for installation of the skeleton. Plastic sheeting was placed on the underside of the exhibit case to prevent the escape of sand into the stand or onto the floor. The plaster cradles for the skull, vertebral column, and ribs were oriented in the case and 2x4 wood spacers were added around the cradles to help keep the sand in position. A thin garnet-colored cloth was lain on top of the cradles to keep the bones from abrading against the cradle and help conceal the white plaster. Hundreds of pounds of playground sand were used to fill the exhibit case. Once it was smoothed into place, a thin top-dressing of garnet abrasive was added to mimic the dirt from Rocky Creek. The remaining ribs from the right side were placed on the sand, as if they had just been removed from the excavation along with the right radius and ulna, which had eroded from the creek bank. David Calame donated a few excavation tools to complete the exhibition.

In closing, I want to briefly note some of the main lessons learned in this process. There are a lot of very specific details to consider. However, maybe it would be useful to step back and talk about strategy, creativity, keeping the final objective in mind, and trying to faithfully reproduce the field excavation. Overall, there should always be a goal of trying to keep the specimens available for future study, rather than buried in plaster.

Finally, fossil preparation is the process of removing a fossil from the surrounding sediment and preserving the specimen so that it may be used for research and/or display. Preparators try to use archival materials, such as acid-free paper, India ink, and reversible glues, that will not degrade over time and cause damage to the specimen. A museum should focus on preserving the long-term stability of specimens and their associated data, so that future generations may use them for research and education.

Figure 4. Attaching the pedestal for the right scapula to the rib cradle.

LIST OF AUTHORS

Kenneth Bader
Osteology Lab Manager, Vertebrate Paleontology Laboratory,
Jackson School of Geosciences, The University of Texas at Austin

David L. Calame, Sr.,
Texas Borderlands Archaeology

Thomas R. Hester, Ph.D.,
Professor emeritus, The University of Texas at Austin,
Member, Board of Directors, The Falls on the Colorado Museum

Jeff M. Martin, Ph.D.,
Assistant Professor of Natural Resource Management
and Extension Bison Specialist, South Dakota State University

Raymond P. Mauldin, Ph.D.,
Center for Archaeological Research,
The University of Texas at San Antonio

Ryan J. Murray,
Editor/publisher of Texas Cache magazine

Harry J. Shafer, Ph.D.,
Professor emeritus, Texas A&M University,
Curator of Archaeology, Witte Museum, San Antonio.

Darlene F. Oostermeyer,
Vice Chairman, Board of Directors,
The Falls on the Colorado Museum, Marble Falls.

www.ingramcontent.com/pod-product-compliance
Lightning Source LLC
Chambersburg PA
CBHW042006150426
43194CB00003B/148